HOW TO KNIT IN THE WOODS

HOW TO KNIT IN THE WOODS

20 Projects for the Great Outdoors

SHANNON OKEY

PHOTOGRAPHY BY RAE NESTER AND KATE BALDWIN

SKIPSTONE

Published by Skipstone, an imprint of The Mountaineers Books
Printed in China

First printing 2008
10 09 08 07   5 4 3 2 1

Copy Editor: Liz McGehee
Design and illustrations: Mayumi Thompson
Charts by Knit Visualizer, knitfoundry.com
Cover photograph: Kate Baldwin
Photographs by Kate Baldwin appear on pages 17, 23, 24, 27, 36, 56, 61, 92, 110, 112, and 115.
Photographs by Rae Nester appear on pages 2, 8, 33, 45, 47, 52, 66, 67, 69, 70, 72, 75, 78, 79, 81, 84, 87, 90, 95, 98, 100, 104, and 107. Photographs by Christine Okey appear on pages 10, 49, 54, 59, 74, 85, 114, and 120.

978-1-59485-088-2

Library of Congress Cataloging-in-Publication Data
Okey, Shannon, 1975-
  How to knit in the woods : 20 projects for the great outdoors /
Shannon Okey.
     p. cm.
  Includes index.
  ISBN 978-1-59485-088-2
  1. Knitting—Patterns. 2. Outdoor recreation—Equipment and supplies.
I. Title.

TT825.O378 2008
746.43'2041—dc22
                    2007052425

Skipstone books may be purchased for corporate, educational, or other promotional sales. For special discounts and information, contact our Sales Department at 800-553-4453 or mbooks@mountaineersbooks.org.

Skipstone
1001 SW Klickitat Way
Suite 201
Seattle, Washington 98134
206.223.6303
www.skipstonepress.org
www.mountaineersbooks.org

LIVE LIFE. MAKE RIPPLES.

CONTENTS

Head to Toe

Staying Clean and Comfortable

Al Fresco Dining

DEDICATION

To my cousins Ethan, Adam, and Harris Hardy, who were off climbing Katahdin while we were lounging around on Vinalhaven, and to my cousin Ivar (aka David Schloz), a better kayaker than I'll ever be!

INTRODUCTION

Knitting is a highly portable, satisfying activity perfect for active hikers and campers. After all, you need something to do around the campfire after a long day of kayaking or climbing! If you're currently longing for the woods, these patterns are fun to knit wherever you are, giving you something tangible to look forward to the next time you make it out of the city. Even if you're more of a backyard camper, you'll find these designs are suited to year-round use at home.

There's more here than just garments, too. This book also includes useful campside tools, such as marshmallow-stick holders and cooler hammocks. There's a combination place mat/cutlery roll to keep your silverware from rattling around the pack or picnic basket, a towel that can be tied to the nearest branch for easy drip-drying, a washcloth that holds either an entire bar of soap or plenty of slivers to make the most of your scraps. . . . In short, you'll find plenty of useful, pretty items that are simple to knit and use.

KNITTING ON THE GO: WHY KNIT IN THE WOODS?

Why knit in the woods? There's something peaceful about knitting that's just suited to the outdoors. It's portable, as mentioned above, and it doesn't require electricity, a WiFi signal, or even a bright light. (Several patterns in this book intentionally include a lot of plain stockinette stitch to make them easy to knit when you're working by firelight.)

Knitting can keep you entertained even if you're stuck in the tent during a rainstorm or waiting for other hikers to catch up on a tough trail. Elizabeth Zimmerman, the inspiration for many modern knitters and the author of numerous books, frequently wrote about outdoor activities and the items she knit while camping and boating. (If I remember correctly, she even mentioned that knitting needles can serve, in a pinch, for a replacement outboard motor part! Who says knitters aren't resourceful?)

Knitting is also a great activity to introduce to others while you're sharing some outdoor time together. Are your kids bored without video games and cable TV? Bring a few spare sets of needles and yarn and show them how fun knitting can be! Or, if you're really clever, get your significant other hooked and you'll never hear a word about how much money you spend on yarn again.

Not just low-tech but supremely easy to pack into your bag and go, knitting in the woods makes a lot of sense!

PACKING LIGHTLY

Here are some how-to ideas for stashing needles, yarn, and other needed materials without taking up too much room in your pack. If you don't have a small, reusable zip pouch for tools, I suggest Lexie Barnes' Mini pouches (available at lexiebarnes.com). They're big enough to contain all the tools listed below plus a few circular needles. Importantly, they have a waterproof exterior coating as well as brightly colored interiors that make finding something as small as a stitch marker or tapestry needle simple in low light.

Circular needles are used in many patterns throughout the book for several reasons. They're used for knitting in the round (their intended purpose), of course, but also because they tend to be easier on the wrists and forearms than straight needles. This may not seem like much of a bonus until you've paddled several miles in your kayak or canoe and just want to knit a few rows before collapsing for the night! Circulars are shorter than straight needles (the needle tips themselves are only 4" to 6" long, depending on brand), and the cables can be wound into a small bundle for storage. Circulars can substitute for double-pointed needles in many circumstances, and pulling the stitches down onto the cable keeps them from going anywhere. You can fit a few pairs of circulars and all the accessories below into one small Lexie Barnes Mini with no problem at all.

NEEDLES AND TOOLS

Bring only the knitting needle sizes you need for planned projects and the following tools, which can save your project when you're miles away from the nearest yarn store: a crochet hook for picking up dropped stitches, a blunt-tipped tapestry needle, three or four clip-style stitch markers, and point protectors for your needles.

Blunt tapestry needles can be used for a variety of things, including threading waste yarn into live stitches (in case you want to try something on without binding off the stitches first), weaving in ends, or even temporarily stitching together a hole in your hat or sweater.

Clip-style stitch markers close at the ends like a safety pin, distinguishing them from their plastic-circle counterparts. If you drop a stitch by the light of your campfire and can't see clearly to pick it up with your crochet hook, catch the loose end of the stitch inside the stitch marker and pin it to its neighboring stitches. You can continue to knit without fear.

The dropped stitch will still be there in the morning and you'll be able to pick it up with your crochet hook then. This also comes in handy when working with "slippery" yarns like the bamboo used in the Tai Shan Hoodie (page 37) or dark-colored yarns that can't be seen well in low light.

If you're working a cable pattern, bring a single double-pointed needle or short circular needle to use as a cable needle. They're less likely to get lost in your bag than a small cable needle.

Point protectors are a must-have if you knit on straight needles: they keep your stitches from falling off the needle tips when you put your project down for the night or pack it into your bag.

WORKING IN LOW LIGHT

Wonder why I keep harping on using certain tools in low-light situations? If you're accustomed to working directly under a lamp or other artificial light or if you have less than perfect vision, you may find it difficult to knit in low light. Heavily shaded tree cover, twilight, firelight? Unless you're knitting fluorescent green yarn or using those new needles that light up, being able to see and use your tools effectively is important. Keep this in mind, too, when choosing projects to bring on a camping trip. Lots of stockinette? Buy one of the yarn bags that clip to your waist and you can knit *while* you're hiking the trail. Entrelac? Fair Isle? Something requiring lots of close attention may not be the optimal project choice. After all, you want to enjoy your time outside, not spend an hour looking for the black ball of yarn you dropped on the forest floor.

YARN

Knitters have a tendency to overpack. I admit to this tendency myself, looking back on several vacations that featured one bag for my clothes and toothbrush and one just for the yarn! Unless you're knitting something that involves multiple yarns at once, such as stranded color work, you don't need to pack every single yarn in your stash. And even if you do, you may want to rethink that project choice (see "Working in Low Light" on page 11). Realistically estimate the number of skeins or balls you'll need while you're gone and select accordingly. If a hat takes you two weeks to knit, bringing enough yarn for a sweater is madness!

There are no center-pull ball winders in the woods (and if you're actually considering packing one, even I can't help you pack lighter!), so wind off hanks and nonball put-ups before you leave. You don't want to spend several hours winding yarn off a series of tree branches only to discover they were covered in poison ivy!

Once you've got a realistic quantity of yarn wound and set aside, slip the balls inside a zip-and-seal freezer bag, leaving an inch or so open to press out the air. You'll be amazed at how much of a center-pull ball is filled with empty airspace! Press down on the yarn from above to eliminate the maximum amount of air. The bag will go flat and compress the yarn into a smaller area without hurting it one bit. Advantages to this system are many, including keeping the yarn dry if there's rain or it slips out of your canoe, plus you can knit camp-side with the yarn still in its bag, keeping it free of twigs, dirt, etc.

You can also use the plastic-bag vacuum trick to make any fabric items smaller, from knit-projects-in-progress to your dirty (or clean!) clothes. It's great when you're carrying a backpack with limited interior space. Use freezer bags instead of regular ones; the plastic is thicker and they can be reused many times. If you're hiking in an area that requires you to carry out all your trash, they also make good temporary receptacles for damp or smelly garbage. Don't forget to remove your knitting first!

CHOOSING YARN FOR OUTDOOR ACTIVITIES

Choosing yarn for projects that will get lots of use outdoors should take into consideration qualities such as durability, waterproofness, and warmth. Read a typical suggested packing list for mountain climbing or kayaking excursions, for example. Wearing jeans on anything other than a short day-trip is not recommended because, among other reasons, cotton doesn't trap heat well, dries poorly once wet, and has a tendency to shrink.

On the other hand, wool works as well or better than most synthetic fibers in a number of categories. It can absorb a considerable amount of water before it actually feels cold on your skin, it holds in heat even when wet (there's a reason fishermen's ganseys were invented for and popularized by actual fishermen!), and it's rugged even in tough conditions. The very best commercial hiking and running socks aren't made of modern miracle fibers, but of soft, lustrous merino wool.

What if you're sensitive to wool or knitting for someone who is? Many people who believe they have a wool allergy have simply not been exposed to quality wool fiber. This is not to discount the knitters out there who actually are allergic to animal-fiber yarns, but studies have shown that only a very small percentage of those who believe they are allergic to wool are. Commercially knit garments too often use very cheap grades of wool, including wool that would be better off left to the rugmakers, and fiber treated with very harsh chemicals to bleach, dye, or make it machine-washable. There's a reason some sweaters are only $19.95 at the department store! Try knitting with 100% merino wool that has not been overly processed. (The wool yarn featured in the dog sweater on page 51 and the hat on page 83 is a high-quality organic merino wool.) Or select a wool-blend yarn to get the best of both worlds.

Bamboo is a plant fiber that's taken the knitting world by storm. Seen in the Tai Shan Hoodie on page 37 and the Cougar Mountain Socks on page 74, bamboo is an environmentally friendly yarn made from ultrarenewable woody plants that don't require nearly as much fertilizer or water to grow as cotton or other plant yarns. It's a great warm-weather knitting fiber because it actively wicks heat and moisture away from the skin.

If you really want to bring the woods into your knitting, look for lyocell-blend (brand name: Tencel) yarns. Tencel is made from wood pulp, but you'd never know it! As an addition to many high-end fabrics, you may already have some in your wardrobe.

Most cotton yarns used in these projects are organic. Why? Because in addition to the environmental concerns mentioned above, organic cotton is soft, beautiful, and can even be purchased in naturally colored shades that require no dye to produce.

Are you definitely allergic to wool? You don't have to resort to cheap acrylic yarns for your knitting. There is a wide range of other plant fiber yarns that work well for outdoorsy projects, among them soy fiber-based yarns, silks, even a new fiber called SeaCell® that's made from seaweed! Hemp yarns make an appearance in several patterns here because hemp wears well and stands up to heavy abuse, something you should look for in all your outdoor gear.

KNITTING REFRESHER COURSE

If you haven't knitted in a while, you may need a quick refresher on materials and terms. Yarn labels in particular have changed quite a bit in the past five years as more manufacturers adopt the Craft Yarn Council of America's standards in labeling and European companies change their standard ball sizes to conform to uniform weights.

READING YARN LABELS

When substituting yarns in patterns, the most important thing to do is make a test swatch. Although the following chart will give you general guidelines for matching the correct needle size to your yarn, everyone knits very differently, which affects the gauge.

Gauge, sometimes called *tension*, is a measurement of the number of stitches in a given inch or sometimes 4 inches (20 centimeters). Where important, row gauge (the number of rows in an inch of stitches) is also given. It's important to do a gauge swatch, a sample of your chosen yarn using the appropriate needle size, before starting any large project. Many knitters don't like to "waste" time doing swatches, but consider the consequences. Why knit for many, many hours only to have a badly fitting or inappropriately sized project?

My gauge swatch may measure 16 stitches per 4 inches using a size 8 needle and a worsted-weight yarn; you could knit the exact same yarn using the exact same needle and get 20 stitches per 4 inches. In a scarf, this isn't a big deal, but in a sweater, you may end up with something that would better fit a dwarf! Unless gauge is not given or is not considered important, work to achieve the gauge given, switching needle sizes if necessary to get the correct gauge.

CYCA'S STANDARD YARN WEIGHT SYSTEM

Yarn weight symbol and category names		Types of yarn	Knit gauge in stockinette stitch per 4 inches	Recommended needle (US sizes)	Recommended needle (metric sizes)
Super Fine	1	Sock, fingering, baby	27–32 sts	1 to 3	2.25–3.24 mm
Fine	2	Sport, baby	23–26 sts	3 to 5	3.25–3.75 mm
Light	3	DK, light worsted	21–24 sts	5 to 7	3.75–4.5 mm
Medium	4	Worsted, afghan, Aran	16–20 sts	7 to 9	4.5–5.5 mm
Bulky	5	Chunky, craft, rug	12–15 sts	9 to 11	5.5–8 mm
Super Bulky	6	Bulky, roving	6–11 sts	11 and larger	8 mm and larger

NEEDLES

Needles are the essential tools for knitting. Most needles you'll see these days are made from plastic, wood, bamboo, or metal. Straight needles are a matched set of long, smooth needles that are pointy on one end, with a knob or button on the other. Circular needles, which are connected in the center by a plastic cord, have a lot of advantages over straight

U.S. NEEDLE SIZE	METRIC NEEDLE SIZE
1	2.25 mm
2	2.75 mm
3	3.25 mm
4	3.5 mm
5	3.75 mm
6	4 mm
7	4.5 mm
8	5 mm
9	5.5 mm
10	6 mm
10½	6.5 mm
11	8 mm
13	9 mm
15	10 mm
17	12.75 mm
19	15 mm
35	19 mm
50	25 mm

needles (see "Packing Lightly" on page 9). DPNs, or double-pointed needles, are straight but pointy at both ends. These are used to knit small tubes that are much smaller than circulars can manage. They are often used for sweater cuffs and socks, but can also be put to work on small tubes of all kinds or in finishing off tight circles (the Ell Pond Nalgene Cozy uses DPNs, and so do both hats).

Needles come in various sizes, and their packaging will usually list both U.S. and metric sizes. Below is a conversion chart for the two measuring systems, but if you've inherited a large number of un- marked needles from a loved one, invest in a needle sizer. These are pieces of metal or plastic with holes in them and are avail- able at yarn stores. After you determine each needle's size, mark it on the end of the needle or on its tip with nail polish or a permanent marker. Different manufacturers' brands, particularly older needles, can sometimes vary widely in size. And if there's any doubt which country your needles are from (was your needle bequeather from the United Kingdom or Australia?), be sure to double-check! It will save much frustration and gauge swatching.

READING PATTERNS

It's important to read through the entire pattern before you start knitting, paying special attention to the information at the beginning, including what yarn was used for the item, which needle sizes and accessories you'll need, gauge, and any notes from the pattern designer with special or unusual things you should notice before knitting the project. If a pattern uses multiple colors, for example, they are indicated by MC (main color) and CC (contrasting color) in the pattern. Asterisks (*) tell you

to repeat the set of directions they enclose. But these are only some of many abbreviations. The most common ones are listed below. Any special stitch patterns or directions will also be listed at the beginning of the pattern.

HELPFUL TECHNIQUES

If you haven't knitted in a while, you may need a quick refresher on materials and some of the techniques used in these patterns. Yarn labels in particular have changed quite a bit in the past five years as more manufacturers adopt the Craft Yarn Council of America's yarn standards in labeling and European companies change their standard ball sizes to conform to certain uniform weights.

KNITTING ABBREVIATIONS

* * repeat directions between *s as many times as indicated

alt	alternate		patt[s]	pattern[s]
approx	approximately		PM	place (stitch) marker
beg	begin[ning]		psso	pass slipped stitch[es] over
BO	bind off [cast off]		pw	purlwise
cab	cable		rem	remain[ing]
CC	contrasting color		rep[s]	repeat[s]
cn	cable needle		rev St st	reverse stockinette stitch
CO	cast on		RH	right hand
cm	centimeter[s]		RS	right side[s]
cont	continue, continuing		rnd[s]	round[s]
dec	decrease, decreasing		sc	single crochet
DPN[s]	double-pointed needles[s]		SKP	slip one stitch, knit one stitch,
foll	follow[s][ing]			pass the slipped stitch over the
g	gram[s]			knitted stitch (decrease)
hdc[s]	half double crochet[s]		SM	slip (stitch) marker
inc	increase, increasing		SSK	slip two stitches as if to knit, knit
K	knit			two stitches together (decrease)
K1f&b	knit in the front and back of the		sl	slip
	next stitch (increase)		slp	slip one as if to purl
Ktbl	knit through back of loop		sl st	slip stitch
K2tog	knit two stitches together		st[s]	stitch[es]
	(decrease)		St st	stockinette stitch
LH	left hand		tbl	through back of loop[s]
m	meter[s]		tog	together
MC	main color		WS	wrong side[s]
M1	make one stitch (increase)		wyif	with yarn in front (of stitches)
mm	millimeter[s]		yd[s]	yard[s]
oz	ounce[s]		YF	yarn forward (to right side of
P	purl			knitting)
Ptbl	purl through back of loop		YB	yarn back (to wrong side of
P2tog	purl two stitches together			knitting)
	(decrease)		YO	yarn over

THE PROVISIONAL CAST ON

The provisional cast on uses two separate strands of yarn. One will be pulled out and thrown away later; make it a contrasting color so you can clearly pick it out. Cotton yarn, which doesn't shed, is the best choice for the waste yarn. Why use the provisional cast on? It allows you to come back after you've knitted the rest of the piece and knit out in the opposite direction. The hat on page 80 uses provisional cast on to add ribbing to a felted hat because you don't want to felt the ribbing; the bag on page 47 uses it to add a flap after the body's been felted. But provisional cast on is not just for felted projects; it comes in handy many other places as well.

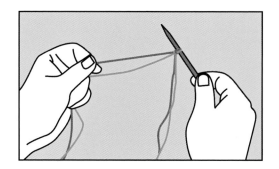

Make a loose slipknot with both strands.

Holding one color around your thumb and one around your finger (just like long-tail, except you're using two separate strands instead of one doubled back on itself), proceed as for long-tail cast on, making certain the loops you pick up that sit on the needle are the yarn you intend to knit with, not the waste yarn.

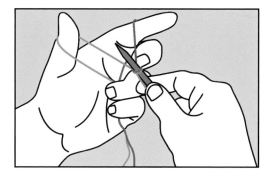

When you reach the end of the row, cut off the contrast color, leaving several inches of spare yarn in case it becomes loose and works its way out before you want it to.

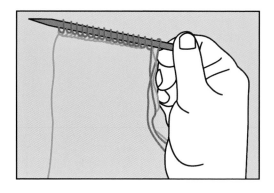

The contrast color will seem to weave along the bottom of the actual stitches. When it's time to take out the waste yarn, take a tapestry needle and pick out the contrast color, slipping the loose loops onto a spare circular needle as you go along.

If you can't master this technique, you have two alternatives: crochet a chain of waste yarn with as many chains as the number of stitches you need and pick up the chains with your knitting needle (you can pull out the chain as needed), or even simpler, cast on and knit three or four rows with your waste yarn, then cut it and pull it out as needed.

I-CORD

I-cord is a tiny 4-stitch tube knit on DPNs. It is used in Picnic Place Mats, page 113. It is very simple to knit and comes in handy for many types of patterns and as a decorative element. You will only need 2 DPNs.

1. Cast on 4 stitches
2. Knit
3. Instead of turning needle to knit back in the other direction, slide stitches to right side of needle and knit row again.
4. Continue as above (the first inch will look a little strange, be patient!), pulling cord as you go to create rounded tube.

THREE-NEEDLE BIND OFF

The three-needle bind off is a method used to simultaneously bind off and seam together two pieces of knitted fabric. It's easy to do and creates a sturdy seam.

1. Line up both needles alongside each other, with the stitches evenly distributed along each one.
2. Using a third needle, insert through the first stitch on each needle as if to knit, then knit the stitches off the needle as if they were one.

3. Repeat step 2, then lift the first stitch on needle 3 over the second one, as in a regular bind off.

4. Continue steps 2 and 3 until all stitches are bound off; break yarn, threading it through the final stitch to close.

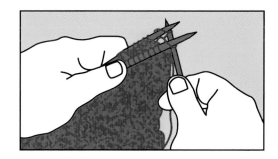

PATTERNS

The patterns in this book have been divided into five sections: Useful Garments, Just Like Home, Head to Toe, Staying Clean and Comfortable, and Al Fresco Dining. In the "Useful Garments" category are two amazing sweaters, one a heavyweight cardigan for colder climes with enough cabled texture to trap body heat effectively and keep you warm and dry, and one lighter-weight midseason hoodie that's great for fall and spring or even a chilly summer night. The hiker's tote is big enough to carry essentials for a day trip or function as a city handbag,

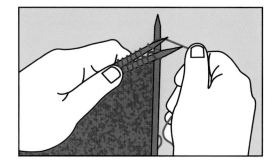

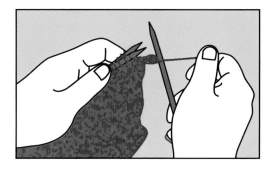

and the dog sweater pattern is easily customizable for your favorite canine companion.

In "Just Like Home," relax with a combination cushion/pillow that's perfect for sleeping bag and camp chair both, and a lace camp stool that folds flat for easy transport and storage. Jillian Moreno's Snowshoe Camping Blanket is thick and soft, perfect for keeping warm in your tent or snuggling on the couch at home, and the recycled sweater lap blanket is a great way to put old sweaters to use (or give you an excuse to knit lots of easy-to-transport, stash-busting squares).

Moms everywhere know that toasty heads and feet make a huge difference when you're outside, but Ariel Altaras has outdone herself with two pairs of beautiful socks worthy of showing off anywhere, not just in the great outdoors. Don't blame us if you want to wear Birkenstocks or clogs year-round to show them off! A cabled hat; a unique felted plus knit-rib hat; and double-knit, extra-thick mittens will make sure all your extremities stay frostbite-free and fashionable.

Although "Staying Clean and Comfortable" says it all about what you'll find in that pattern section, you'll appreciate both form and function, from a tough yet soft hemp towel to a soap-saving washcloth and knitted inserts to make any pair of hiking boots comfier.

"Al Fresco Eating," the final section, discourages bears and ants, burns, dehydration, and errant forks stabbing through your backpack. Get that cooler off the ground and into the air using Minnie Olson's cooler hammock (you never know when an army of ants might invade). Marshmallow-stick holders can be used as pot holders at home with the addition of simple cotton batting, and a wool Nalgene cozy keeps your cool water cooler. Finally, camp place mats that double as rolls for your silverware and utensils add style, as well as a practical bit of padding and organization, to your campsite (or dining room table!).

USEFUL GARMENTS

Some outdoor gear lacks a certain bit of flair, but not these patterns. Whether you're sea kayaking in Maine or camping in Oregon, the fisherman-style cable-knit sweater called Snake in the Woods will keep you warm and more-or-less dry, even in damp conditions. The Tai Shan Hoodie will add warmth and style to any adventure, and you won't want to leave home without your Yodel Hiker's Tote, filled with all those outdoor essentials. There's even a sweater for Fido!

SNAKE IN THE WOODS CARDIGAN
BY SHANNON OKEY AND JOHN PUDDICK

This cardigan was designed by Shannon and knit by John Puddick, a veteran Aran sweater knitter with more than fifty to his name. It depicts double snakes twisted around each other on either side of the button band and *ouroboros,* or snakes swallowing their tails, around the cuffs and bottom welt. This sweater uses an unusual performance yarn that protects the wearer under even the snowiest or wettest conditions. Dale of Norway Hauk is a beautiful, durable wool yarn that has been treated with Teflon to increase its water-shedding properties—yes, the same polymer used to coat nonstick pans! However, with a soft hand and beautiful drape, you'd never guess this yarn is every bit as high-tech as any $500 ski jacket!

SIZE

Men's, One size

This is also an excellent sweater for women—make the arms slightly shorter if desired, and change the position of the buttonholes.

FINISHED MEASUREMENTS

Chest: 48"

MATERIALS

15 balls of Hauk from Dale of Norway (100% wool; 109 yds; 50 g) in color 0004 Gray

US sizes 5 (3.75 mm) and 3 (3.25 mm) straight needles or sizes needed to obtain gauge

Cable needle

Stitch holder

10 buttons

Tapestry needle

Charts (download from www.skipstonebooks .org or www.knitgrrl.com)

GAUGE

30 sts = 4" (10 cm) in St st with larger needles

POD RIBBING PATTERN

Row 1 (RS): Work (K1tbl, YO, K1tbl) in next st—3 sts.

Row 2: P1, K1tbl, P1.

Row 3: K1, work (K1tbl, YO, K1tbl) in next st, K1—5 sts.

Row 4: P2, K1tbl, P2.

Row 5: K2, P1, K2.

Row 6: P2, K1tbl, P2.

Row 7: K2, P1, K2.

Row 8: P5.

Row 9: K1, K3tog—3 sts.

Row 10: P3.

Row 11: K3tog—1 st.

Row 12: P1tbl.

Row 13: K1tbl.

Row 14: P1tbl.

Rep Rows 1–14 for patt.

BACK

See Welt Chart

WELT

With larger needles CO 2 sts.

Row 1 (RS): P12, K2, P1, work (K1tbl, YO, K1tbl) in next st, P9, K2—29 sts.

Row 2: Wyif sl 1, P1, K9, P3, K1, P2, K12.

Begin Welt Chart, working rows 1–20 of chart 7 times.

After completing 7th repeat of row 20 (142 rows total from beg), work rows 21 & 22 of Welt Chart.

Bind off, keeping in patt as follows: P12, K2, P1, K3tog, P9, K2. Leave last st on needle, do not cut yarn.

BODY

With RS facing, insert point of RH needle under first selvedge st on long side of welt. K1, bind off last st of welt (1 st on needle). Pick up and knit 73 more sts along selvedge—74 sts.

FOUNDATION ROWS

Row 1 (WS): Kf&b into each st across to last st, K1—147 sts.

Row 2: K1, P4, K1tbl, [P3, K1tbl] 34 times, P4, K1.

Row 3: K5, P1tbl, [K3, P1tbl] 34 times, K5.

BEGIN PATTERN

Row 1 (RS): K1, p4, [K1tbl, P3] 3 times, *work row 1 of Pod Ribbing, P3, [K1tbl, P3] 3 times; rep from * to last 2 sts, P1, K1—163 sts.

Row 2: K5, [P1tbl, K3] 3 times, *work row 2 of Pod Ribbing, K3, [P1tbl, K3] 3 times; rep to last 2 sts, K2.

Continue as established, beginning and ending RS rows as for row 1 and WS rows as for row 2, working rows 3–14 of Pod Ribbing as appropriate—147 sts.

Row 15 (RS): K1, P4, K1tbl, P3, *work row 1 of Pod Ribbing, P3, [K1tbl, P3] 3 times, rep from * to last 10 sts, work row 1 of Pod Ribbing, P3, K1tbl, P4, K1—165 sts.

Row 16: K5, P1tbl, K3, work row 2 of Pod Ribbing, *[K3, P1tbl] 3 times, K3, work row 2 of Pod Ribbing; rep from * to last 9 sts, K3, P1tbl, K5.

Continue as established, beginning and ending RS rows as for row 15 and WS rows as for row 16, working rows 3–14 of Pod Ribbing as appropriate, last row worked is row 28—147 sts.

Rep rows 1–28 twice more, then rows 1–4 once—98 rows.

Rows 99–110: Continue in patt, omitting first and last repeat of Pod Ribbing on each row, replacing st on RS rows with K1tbl, and on WS rows with P1tbl.

SHAPE RAGLAN ARMHOLES

Maintaining st patt, bind off 3 sts at beg of next 2 rows.

Dec row (RS): K1, P1, K1tbl, P2tog, P2, work in patt to last 7 sts, P2, P2tog, K1tbl, P1, K1.

Next row: K2, P1tbl, K3, work in patt to last 6 sts, K3, P1tbl, K2.

Rep last 2 rows 24 times more—89 sts.

Next row: (RS): Rep dec row.

Next row: k2, P1tbl, K2tog, K2, work in patt to last 8 sts, K2, K2tog, P1tbl, K2.

Rep last 2 rows 8 times more—53 sts. Bind off in patt.

LEFT FRONT

WELT

With larger needles, CO 26 sts.

Row 1 (RS): P12, K2, P10, K2.

Row 2: Wyif sl 1, P1, K10, P2, K12.

Row 3: Wyif sl 1, P11, K2, P10, K2.

Row 4: Wyif sl 1, P1, K10, P2, K12.

Rows 5–7: Rep rows 3 & 4 once and row 3 once more.

Row 8: Wyif sl 1, P1, K8, M1, K2, P2, K12—27 sts.

Row 9: Wyif sl 1, P11, K2, P2, K1, P8, K2.

Row 10: Wyif sl 1, P1, K8, M1, P1, K2, P2, K12—28 sts.

Row 11: Wyif sl 1, P11, K2, P2, sl next st to cn, hold to front, P1, K1, knit st from cn, P4, K3, P1, K2.

Rows 12–19: Continue, following Welt Chart.

Row 20: Wyif sl 1, P1, K1, P2, M1, K9, P2, K12—29 sts.

Row 21: Wyif p11, K2, P7, sl next 3 sts to cn, hold to back, K2, (K1, P2) from cn, P1, K2.

Row 22: Wyif sl 1, P1, K3, P3, K7, P2, K12.

Rows 23–28: Work Rows 16–20 of Welt Chart.

Rows 29–68: Work Rows 1–20 of Welt Chart twice.

Rows 69–70: Work Rows 21 & 22 of Welt Chart.

Bind off in patt as for back welt. Working same as for back, pick up a total of 36 sts along welt.

FOUNDATION ROWS

Row 1 (WS): Kf&b into each st across to last st, K1—71 sts.

Row 2: K1, P4, [K1tbl, P3] 13 times, K1tbl, P10, K1tbl, P1, K1.

Row 3: K2, P1tbl, K10, P1tbl, [K3, P1tbl] 13 times, K5.

BEGIN PATTERN

Row 1 (RS): K1, P4, *[K1tbl, P3] 3 times, work row 1 of Pod Ribbing, P3; rep from * twice more, K1tbl, P3, K1tbl, work row 1 of Left Snake Chart (12 sts), work row 1 of Pod Ribbing, P1, K1—79 sts.

Row 2: K2, work row 2 of Pod Ribbing, work row 2 of Left Snake Chart, P1tbl, K3, P1tbl, *work row 2 of Pod Ribbing, K3, [P1tbl, K3] 3 times, rep from * to last 2 sts, K2.

Continue as established, rep rows 1–14 for Pod Ribbing and Pod Chart as follows: to end of row 28 once, then 29–52 to end of row 98—77 sts.

Rows 99–110: Omit first rep of Pod Ribbing as for back.

SHAPE RAGLAN ARMHOLES

Maintaining st patt, bind off 3 sts at beg of next row. Work next row in patt.

Dec row (RS): K1, P1, K1tbl, P2tog, P2, work in patt to end.

Next row: Work in patt to last 6 sts, K3, P1tbl, K2.

Rep last 2 rows 24 times more—48 sts.

Next row (RS): Rep dec row.

AT THE SAME TIME, continue working Left Snake Chart up the front panel, ending with a row 53, approximately 5 or 6 inches shorter than the competed back.

Continuing in patt for the rest of the piece, place the knit sts that make up the body of the two snakes on stitch holders or waste yarn, and work the remaining sts of the snake panel in rev St st throughout.

Once the front is finished, working with 2 sts at a time, work 3 inches of St st and then make the snake head as follows:

Row 1: Knit into the front, back, front of the next st, M1, knit into the front, back, and front again of the last st—7 sts.

Row 2: Purl.

Row 3: Knit.

Row 4: Purl.

Row 5: SSK, K3, K2tog—5 sts.

Row 6: Purl.

Row 7: SSK, k1, k2tog–3 sts.

Row 8: Purl.

Row 9: K3tog. Cut yarn and pull end through last st.

Repeat this for the second snake and then sew them down using a whipstitch, so that they are pointing towards the shoulder seam.

Next row: Bind off 5 sts, work in patt to last 8 sts, K3tog, K2tog, P1tbl, K2.

Next row: Rep dec row.

Next row: Bind off 5 sts, work in patt to last 8 sts, K3tog, K2tog, P1tbl, K2.

Next row: K1, P1, K1tbl, P2tog, P2, work in patt to last 2 sts, K2tog.

Next row: P2tog, work in patt to last 8 sts, K3, K2tog, P1tbl, K2.

Rep last 2 rows until 5 sts remain.

Next row (RS): K1, P1, K1tbl, P2tog.

Next row: P2tog tbl, K2.

Next row: K1, K2tog.

Next row: K2tog. Fasten off.

RIGHT FRONT

With larger needles, CO 29 sts.

Row 1 (RS): P12, K2, P1, work (K1tbl, YO, K1tbl) in next st, P9, K2.

Row 2: Wyif sl 1, P1, K9, P3, K1, P2, K12.

Follow rows 1–20 of Welt Chart twice, then rows 21–52 once.

Next row: Wyif sl 1, P11, K2, P2, P2tog, P7, K2.

Next row: Wyif sl 1, P1, K10, P2, K12.

Bind off in patt as for back.

Continue as for Left Front, reversing all shaping and using Right Snake Chart.

SLEEVES (MAKE 2)

CO 29 sts and work rows 1–20 of welt chart 2 times, then rows 21–45—64 total rows. Bind off loosely in patt leaving the last st on the needle.

CO 33 more sts in the same manner as for the back and front welts, evenly across the sleeve—34 sts.

Row 1: Kf&b in every st to last st, K1—67 sts.

Row 2: K1, (K1tbl, P3) 16 times, K1tbl, K1.

Row 3: K1, (P1tbl, K3) 16 times, P1tbl, K1.

Row 4: K1, (K1tbl, P3) 2 times, place Pod Ribbing row 1, P3, * (K1tbl, P3) 3 times, place Pod Ribbing row 1; rep to end.

Row 5: K1, (P1tbl, K3) twice, place Pod Ribbing row 2, K3, *(P1tbl, K3) 3 times, place Pod Ribbing row 2; repeat from * twice, then (K3, P1tbl) twice, K1.

Continue in patt placing Pod Ribbing rows the same as the back, AT THE SAME TIME, on row 16 and every following 6th row, increase 1 st at the beg and end of the row. Make sure to incorporate extra pods as the patt allows, until you have 99 sts.

SHAPE ARMHOLES

With RS facing, bind off 3 sts at beginning of next 2 rows.

SHAPE RAGLAN

Row 1: K1, P1, K1tbl, P2tog, P2, patt to last 7 sts, P2, P2tog, K1tbl, P1, K1—91 sts.

Row 2: K2, P1tbl, K3, patt to last 6 sts, K3, P1tbl, K2.

Repeat these two rows until there are 39 sts.

With RS facing:

Row 1: K1, P1, K1tbl, P2tog, P2, patt to last 7 sts, P2, P2tog, K1tbl, P1, K1.

Row 2: K2, P1tbl, K2tog, K2, patt to last 7 sts, K2, K2tog, P1tbl, K2 until 13 sts remain.

Bind off in patt, incorporating decreases.

FINISHING

Join back, fronts, and sleeves; sew sleeve and side seams.

LEFT FRONT BAND

With smaller needles, CO 10 sts.

Row 1: Pick up 1 st as if to purl from edge of sweater—11 sts. Working picked up st tog with first st of row, [K1, P1] 4 times, K2.

Row 2: [K1, P1] 5 times.

Rep last 2 rows twice.

***Begin buttonhole:** Continuing to pick up sts as before, K1, P1, K1, bind off 3 sts, P1, K2.

Complete buttonhole: [K1, P1] twice, turn, cast on 4 sts, turn. Sl next st on to RH needle, bind off last cast on st, sl st back to LH needle, purl that st, K1, P1.

Rep rows 1 & 2 9 times. Rep from * 8 times more.

Last buttonhole: Rep buttonhole rows. Rep rows 1 & 2 once, then row 1 once more. Bind off 4 sts, leave rem 6 sts on a holder.

RIGHT FRONT BAND

With RS facing and smaller needles, pick up 1 st from edge of sweater. CO 9 sts—10 sts.

Row 1 (RS): K2, [P1, P1] 4 times.

Row 2: [P1, K1] 5 times. Pick up st from edge of sweater, pull last st on needle over new st—10 sts.

Rep rows 1 & 2 to end of band. Bind off 4 sts, leave rem 6 sts on a holder.

NECK BAND

With larger needles, pick up and knit 147 sts around neck edge, beg and ending with sts on holders at top of bands.

Next row: Dec 24 sts evenly around band—123 sts. Work in [K1, P1] ribbing (ending with K1) for 1″. Change to smaller needles and work for 1″ more.

Fold neck band forward to RS, sew sides of band closed. Turn band to WS and tack long edge of band to inside of sweater.

Weave in ends, block.

TAI SHAN HOODIE

BY ANDI MOON SMITH FOR KNIT BRIT

This hooded sweater is named after a famous panda born at the Smithsonian National Zoological Park (commonly known as the National Zoo) in Washington, D.C., in 2005. While his real name is Tai Shan, which means "peaceful mountain," he's also known as Butterstick. This hoodie's bamboo yarn is slippery soft like butter, and pandas eat bamboo, so the name seems apropos! Bamboo yarn is made from ultrarenewable bamboo, which grows quickly and with less fertilizer and water than cotton and other fiber-producing plants. Don't be surprised to see it popping up in housewares and accessories at the local department store, too. Its weight and drape make any pattern look elegant, and its ability to warm you up (or keep you cool in the heat) with a lightweight fabric makes it quite a miracle fiber!

U.S. SIZE (IN)

1 (2, 3, 4, 5)

32–34 (36–38, 40–42, 44–46, 48–50)

METRIC SIZE (CM)

1 (2, 3, 4, 5)

81–86 (91–96, 102–107, 112–117, 123–127)

FINISHED MEASUREMENTS

Bust (actual): 36 (40, 44, 48, 52)" [91 (102, 112, 123, 132) cm]

Waist: 32 (36, 40, 44, 48)" [81 (91, 102, 112, 123) cm]

Bottom: 56 (60, 64, 68, 72)" [56 (60, 64, 68, 72) cm]

Overall length: 26 (27, 27, 28, 28)" [66 (69, 69, 71, 71) cm]

Sleeves: 27 (27½, 27½, 28, 28)" [69 (70, 70, 71, 71) cm]

Armhole to cuff: 17 (17½, 17½, 18, 18)" [43 (44, 44, 46, 46) cm]

Armhole to shoulder: 9 (9½, 9½, 10, 10)" [23 (24, 24, 25, 25) cm]

MATERIALS

7 (8, 9) balls of Bamboo from Southwest Trading Company (100% bamboo; 250 yds; 100 g) in color 126 Black

U.S. size 3 (3.25 mm) needles

1 button, 2" diameter

8 stitch markers

U.S. size F-5 (3.75 mm) crochet hook

Large-eyed, blunt tapestry needle

Straight pins or knit clips for assembly

GAUGE

28 sts and 40 rows = 4" (10 cm) square in
St st

SPECIAL ABBREVIATIONS

Sl 1pw: Slip 1 purlwise.

Kb&f: Knit into back and front of st (similar
to but not the same as K1f&b)

hdc: half double crochet (optional;
see "Note")

NOTE

The half double crochet trim around the edge of the sweater is optional, but does add a little extra weight to the edges, creating a beautiful drape in the piece. See "Resources" at the back of the book for suggested crochet books if you don't already know how to crochet. Also, the oversized vintage 2" (5 cm) Bakelite button from Shannon's collection is not widely available. Not to fear! If you can't find an oversized button you like, the directions tell you how to size the buttonholes for any size button.

BACK

CO 184 (198, 212, 226, 240) sts.

Row 1 (WS): Purl.

Row 2: Knit.

Row 3: Purl.

Row 4: Purl.

Row 5: Knit.

Row 6: Purl.

Work rows 5 and 6 another 3 times, then prepare to work the chevrons by placing markers after the following sts:

Size 1: 8, 28, 36, 56, 148, 156, 176

Size 2: 8, 28, 36, 56, 142, 162, 170, 190

Size 3: 10, 32, 42, 64, 148, 170, 180, 202

Size 4: 10, 32, 42, 64, 150, 172, 182, 204

Size 5: 12, 36, 48, 72, 168, 192, 204, 228

Now work as foll:

Row 1: Knit.

Row 2: Purl.

Row 3: Knit.

Row 4: Purl.

Row 5: *Knit to marker, SM, SSK, knit to 2 sts before next marker, K2tog, SM, rep from * 7 times, knit to end.

Row 6: Purl.

Rep these 6 rows 8 (8, 9, 9, 10) times until 144 (158, 168, 182, 192) sts rem.

Remove markers.

Cont in St st until back measures 12 (13, 13, 14, 14)" [30 (33, 33, 36, 36) cm] or desired length.

ARMHOLE AND BACK SHAPING

BO 8 sts at beg of next 2 rows—128 (142, 152, 166, 176) sts.

Row 1: K2, SSK, knit to last 4sts, K2tog, K2.

Row 2: Purl.

Row 3: Knit.

Row 4: Purl.

Rep these 4 rows 3 (4, 4, 5, 5) times—122 (134, 144, 156, 166) sts.

Cont armhole shaping and beg center back shaping as foll:

Row 1: K2, SSK, knit to last 4 sts, K2tog, K2.

Row 2: Purl, placing markers after 40/80 (44/88, 48/96, 52/104, 55/110) sts.

Row 3: Knit to st before marker, K1f&b, SM, Kb&f twice, knit to end.

Row 4: Purl.

Rep these 4 rows 5 (5, 5, 6, 6) times—126 (146, 156, 174, 192) sts.

Cont in St st until work measures 25 (26, 26, 27, 27)" [64 (66, 66, 69, 69) cm] or 1" (2.5 cm) less than desired length.

LEFT SHOULDER

Row 1: K73 (85, 87, 97, 107), turn.

Row 2: BO 68 (80, 82, 92, 102) sts, purl to end.

Row 3: Knit.

Row 4: BO 5 sts, purl to end—24 (28, 32, 36, 40) sts.

Work in St st until desired length, then BO.

RIGHT SHOULDER

With RS facing:

Row 1: Knit.

Row 2: Purl.

Row 3: BO 5 sts, knit to end—24 (28, 32, 36, 40) sts.

Work in St st until same length as left shoulder. BO.

LEFT FRONT

CO 92 (100, 106, 114, 120) sts.

Row 1: Purl.

Row 2: Knit.

Row 3: Purl.

Row 4: Purl.

Row 5: Knit.

Row 6: Purl.

Work rows 5 and 6 another 3 times, then prepare to work the chevrons by placing markers after the following sts:

Size 1: 8, 28, 36, 56

Size 2: 8, 28, 36, 56

Size 3: 10, 32, 42, 64

Size 4: 10, 32, 42, 64

Size 5: 12, 36, 48, 72

Now work as foll:

Row 1: Knit.

Row 2: Purl.

Row 3: Knit.

Row 4: Purl.

Row 5: *Knit to marker, SM, SSK, knit to 2 sts before next marker, K2tog, SM, rep from *
once, knit to end.

Row 6: Purl.

Rep these 6 rows 9 (9, 10, 10, 11) more times until 56 (64, 68, 74, 76) sts rem. Remove markers.

Cont working in St st without shaping until front measures 10" (25 cm), then shape bust darts as foll:

Row 1: Knit. Place markers after 22/26 (26/30, 30/34, 34/40, 38/46) sts.

Row 2: Purl.

Row 3: *Knit to st before marker, K1f&b, SM, Kb&f, rep from *, knit to end.

Row 4: Purl.

Work rows 3 and 4 another 3 (3, 4, 4, 5) times—68 (76, 82, 90, 96) sts. Remove markers.

Work without shaping until work measures 12 (13, 13, 14, 14)" [30 (33, 33, 36, 36) cm] or desired length.

ARMHOLE SHAPING

With RS facing, BO 8 sts at beg of row 60—(68, 74, 82, 88) sts.

Purl 1 row, then work as foll:

Row 1: K2, SSK, knit to end.

Row 2: Purl.

Row 3: Knit.

Row 4: Purl.

Rep these 4 rows 3 (4, 4, 5, 5) more times—57 (64, 70, 77, 83) sts.

NECK SHAPING

Row 1: K2, SSK, knit to end.

Row 2: Sl 1pw, P1, psso, purl to end.

Row 3: Knit.

Row 4: Purl.

Rep these 4 rows 10 (10, 11, 11, 12) times—37 (44, 48, 55, 59) sts.

Then dec at neck edge only every other row until 24 (28, 32, 36, 40) sts rem.

Cont in St st until left front is same length as back. BO.

RIGHT FRONT

CO 92 (100, 106, 114, 120) sts.

Row 1: Purl.

Row 2: Knit.

Row 3: Purl.

Row 4: Purl.

Row 5: Knit.

Row 6: Purl.

Work rows 5 and 6 another 3 times, then on last row with WS facing, prepare to work the chevrons by placing markers after the following sts:

Size 1: 8, 28, 36, 56

Size 2: 8, 28, 36, 56

Size 3: 10, 32, 42, 64

Size 4: 10, 32, 42, 64

Size 5: 12, 36, 48, 72

Now work as foll:

Row 1: Knit.

Row 2: Purl.

Row 3: Knit.

Row 4: Purl.

Row 5: *Knit to marker, SM, SSK, knit to 2 sts before next marker, K2tog, SM, rep from *
once, knit to end.

Row 6: Purl.

Rep these 6 rows 9 (9, 10, 10, 11) more times until 56 (64, 68, 74, 76) sts rem. Remove markers.

Cont working in St st without shaping until front measures 10" (25 cm), then shape bust darts as foll:

Row 1: Knit.

Row 2: Purl. Place markers after 22/26 (26/30, 30/34, 34/40, 38/46) sts.

Row 3: *Knit to st before marker, K1f&b, SM, Kb&f, rep from *, knit to end.

Row 4: Purl.

Work rows 3 and 4 another 3 (3, 4, 4, 5) times—68 (76, 82, 90, 96) sts. Remove markers.

Work without shaping until work measures 12 (13, 13, 14, 14)" [30 (33, 33, 36, 36) cm] or desired length.

ARMHOLE SHAPING

With RS facing, BO 8 sts at beg of row—60 (68, 74, 82, 88) sts.

Purl 1 row.

Row 1: Knit to last 4 sts, K2tog, K2.

Row 2: Purl.

Row 3: Knit.

Row 4: Purl.

Rep these 4 rows 3 (4, 4, 5, 5) more times—57 (64, 70, 77, 83) sts.

NECK SHAPING

Row 1: Knit to last 4 sts, K2tog, K2.

Row 2: Sl 1pw, P1, psso, purl to end.

Row 3: Knit.

Row 4: Purl.

Rep these 4 rows 10 (10, 11, 11, 12) times—37 (44, 48, 55, 59) sts.

Then dec at neck edge only every other row until 24 (28, 32, 36, 40) sts rem.

Cont in St st until right front is same length as back and left front. BO.

SLEEVES (MAKE 2)

CO 92 (100, 106, 114, 120) sts.

Row 1: Purl.

Row 2: Knit.

Row 3: Purl.

Row 4: Purl.

Row 5: Knit.

Row 6: Purl.

Work rows 5 and 6 another 3 times, then prepare to work the chevrons by placing markers after 36/56 (40/60, 42/64, 46/68, 48/72) sts. Now work as foll:

Row 1: Knit.

Row 2: Purl.

Row 3: Knit.

Row 4: Purl.

Row 5: Knit to marker, SM, SSK, knit to 2 sts before next marker, K2tog, SM, knit to end.

Row 6: Purl.

Rep these 6 rows 8 (8, 9, 9, 10) times—76 (82, 86, 94, 98)sts.

Remove markers.

Cont in St st until sleeve measures 17 (17½, 17½, 18, 18)" [43 (44, 44, 46, 46) cm]

ARMHOLE SHAPING

BO 8 sts at beg of next 2 rows—60 (66, 70, 78, 82)sts.

Row 1: K2, SSK, knit to last 4 sts, K2tog, K2.

Row 2: Purl.

Row 3: Knit.

Row 4: Purl.

Rep these 4 rows 12 (13, 14, 15, 16) times—34 (36, 40, 46, 48) sts.

Then rep rows 1 and 2 only 2 (3, 3, 4, 4) times—30 (30, 34, 38, 40) sts.

Cont in St st until sleeve measures 26 (27, 27, 28, 28)" [66 (69, 69, 71, 71) cm] or desired length. BO.

HOOD

CO 90 sts and work in St st for 30" (76 cm). BO.

BLOCKING

Lay the pieces out flat; dampen slightly with a spray bottle and stretch into shape. Allow to dry thoroughly before sewing together.

ASSEMBLY

Because this yarn is both a fine weight and relatively heavy (drapey), it can be a little tricky to stitch together unless you are generous with the pins. Small claw clips designed to hold pieces together during seaming are available at many knitting and craft shops (or use small claw-style hair clips). As each piece is pinned or clipped together to its neighbor, carefully stitch using your preferred method, or chain the pieces together on the reverse side using an appropriately sized crochet hook and slip stitch.

BUTTON BAND

Row 1: With bottom of right front facing, using crochet hook, hdc into each edge st along right front, across back, across left front, up left front, across hood, and down right front. Fasten off and work row 1 another 4 times.

BUTTONHOLES

Determine where (and how many) buttonhole(s) will be placed. When you get to the first placement, chain a length equal to width of chosen button(s), skip the same number of hdcs, and then cont in hdc pattern as established. Rep for each buttonhole, working the same number of hdcs into chain-st section of buttonhole.

YODEL HIKER'S TOTE

BY SHANNON OKEY

This backpack-style tote would be equally at home on the hiking trail or the subway. In fact, with a mere change of the straps, it's also a beautifully capacious handbag. Using purchased handles or something as simple as braided I-cord, you can transform the very same design into any number of lovely bags. If you can't find the Grayson leather handles or want unique backpack straps, track down two matching (or mostly matching) leather belts instead.

FINISHED SIZE

Varies according to your washing machine and other factors; bag pictured measures approximately 13" x 10" across bottom after felting

MATERIALS

MC Approx 375 yards or 2 skeins of Cascade 220 from Cascade Yarns (100% wool; 220 yds) in color 2445

CC 1 skein of Malabrigo worsted-weight kettle-dyed merino (100% wool; 216 yds) in color 224 Autumn Forest

Grayson E leather handles, specifically Long Rolled Handles with Buckles, 18½" long, or 2 leather belts

U.S. size 8 (5 mm) circular needle, 16" (41) cm long

Cotton waste yarn (several yards)

Tapestry needle

U.S. size F-5 (3.75 mm) crochet hook

4 stitch markers

GAUGE

Gauge is not critical to this project due to the felted body (see "Note"). Prefelted gauge in sample shown here was 17 sts = 4" (10 cm) and 22 rows = 4" (10 cm)

SPECIAL STITCHES

Seed Stitch

Row 1: *K1, P1*, rep across row.

Row 2: *P1, K1*, rep across row.

Rep rows 1 and 2.

NOTE

If you have never felted before, please knit and felt a small swatch before knitting the main bag body (see "Felting" below). Is the swatch 100% felted? Can you hold it up to the light and see few (if any) pinpricks of light? If there are more holes in the fabric than you might want, switch to the next smallest needle and try again.

PATTERN

CO 100 sts provisionally with cotton waste yarn and MC, PM at sts 15, 35, 15, and 35. Join rnd, taking care not to twist sts.

Knit 5 rnds. Beg inc rnds as foll:

FIRST SET OF INCREASES

Inc rnd: After first marker, K1f&b, knit to st before next marker *K1f&b, SM, K1f&b, knit to st before next marker*, rep from * to * around, end K1f&b.

Knit 5 plain rnds (with no increases).

Rep inc rnd plus 5 plain rnds 3 times.

SECOND SET OF INCREASES

Work inc rnd as above.

>Knit 3 plain rnds.

>Rep inc rnd plus 5 plain rnds 7 times.

>Knit 31 plain rnds.

>**Final rnd:** Removing markers as you knit, BO first 3 sides loosely (both long sides and 1 short one). Do not BO final short side.

Front view, without handles sewn on

BOTTOM SECTION

Knitting back and forth in garter st, knit until bottom reaches other side of bound-off opening (48 ridges), and BO. Do not cut yarn.

With bag turned WS out and using crochet hook, join bottom flap to bound-off sides around bottom opening with a sl st or sc. Don't forget to stitch across side of bottom piece that's already connected to rest of bag; this line of crochet sts will give bottom definition and strength.

FELTING

Weave in ends and felt bag by running it through a hot wash cycle with cold rinse in your washer. Soap is not necessary, but some washers may require more than one cycle to felt completely. Remove bag and dry, upside down, on a vase, coffee can, or appropriately sized box. You may want to stuff the bottom with plastic grocery bags to maintain its shape while drying.

FLAP

Remove cotton waste yarn from provisional CO at bag opening. Sts that were previously trapped inside cotton yarn will be slightly felted but can still be picked up again.

Place sts back on 16" (41 cm) needle and, starting at beg of original rnd with CC, knit around top of bag, binding off as you go on first long side and first short side. Knit across second long side without binding off, then BO rem short side.

One long side's sts (there should be at least 35 sts, though you can also make back flap wider if you like) rem on needle. Cut yarn and return to beg of row. Knit seed st until flap measures 6" (15 cm) and BO in patt.

STRAPS

Using holes drilled into straps, stitch them into place with CC and tapestry needle. It helps to have a partner for this to ensure proper placement. If you are opting to use two old leather belts instead, you may need a sharp awl to drill the needed holes for stitching.

BERWICK DOG SWEATER

BY SHANNON OKEY

This sweater was created for my dog, Anezka, and is related to the Canine Capelet, a design I demonstrated on DIY Network's popular knitting show, *Knitty Gritty*. On the show, the sweater was trimmed in yarn spun from dog fur, but one can only imagine the looks your dog will give you if the yarn isn't made from his or her *own* fur! This is more "recipe" than pattern and can be adapted to a wide range of dog sizes and even many different types of yarns if you're looking to use up lovely leftovers from other projects. Its garter-stitch chest covering will keep your pup's fur free of burrs, and your canine friend will stay warm even when sitting on the cold ground, all while looking stylish.

FINISHED SIZE

Variable (see "Note")

MATERIALS

1 skein of O-Wool Classic from Vermont Organic Fiber Company (100% organic merino wool; 198 yds) in color Cornflower

U.S. size 8 (5 mm) needle, 16" (41 cm) long

3 stitch markers

2 buttons, 1" diameter

Measuring tape

Tapestry needle

Waste yarn

GAUGE

Not critical, but you'll need to do a swatch.

NOTE

Dogs come in a wide range of sizes. Anezka is a long-haired miniature dachshund who's not so miniature, weighing in at 16 pounds. Although her sweater required only one skein of yarn, chances are your dog is larger. Estimate one skein for small dogs, three or more for medium-sized dogs, and four to five for larger dogs. To be on the safe side, purchase yarn from a reputable store that allows returns! Alternately—and this is a great way to clear out lots of small bits and bobs from other projects—knit this sweater using yarns from your stash. The pattern itself is very adaptable to different gauges and yarn styles.

PATTERN

Determine number of sts to CO as foll: knit a 4" x 4" (10 cm x 10 cm) gauge swatch in 3 x 3 rib (*knit 3, purl 3*).

Measure your dog's neck. If the neck is 10" (25 cm) around and you are getting 6 sts to 1" (2.5 cm), CO 60 sts.

CO your determined number of sts.

Place marker. Divide number of sts by 3 and space markers accordingly. With a 60-st CO, for example, place markers every 20 sts. If number cannot be evenly divided, just make sure back st marker is centered between the other two.

Knit 3 x 3 rib for 1" (2.5 cm) (2" or more on larger dogs or dogs with long necks, such as greyhounds).

Beg inc rnds as foll:

Row 1: K1f&b, SM, knit to next marker, *K1f&b, SM, K1f&b, knit to st before next marker*, K1f&b.

Row 2: Knit.

Rep rows 1 and 2 until sweater is wide enough to reach across dog's chest at top of legs.

CHEST FLAP

Knit from beg of rnd to second marker, then slip next ⅔ of sts onto waste yarn and secure.

Knitting back and forth, knit garter st (knit every row) until chest flap covers dog's chest. For smaller or elderly dogs who are prone to shivering or extrasensitive to cold, you can cont knitting so flap covers belly as well.

BUTTON FLAP

At beg of row, CO enough sts to reach from side of dog's chest/belly up to upper back. Here, 15 extra sts were CO. For larger dogs, you will need more. Knit across and CO the same number of new sts on other side.

BUTTONHOLES

Knit back and forth for 5 to 6 rows, depending on size of chosen buttons.

Knit 5 sts in from side and BO as many sts as your buttons are wide; cont to knit to other side and create a second buttonhole, leaving 5 or an equal number of sts on other side of second buttonhole.

Knit across and CO new sts for other side of buttonhole.

Cont knitting for 5 to 6 rows. BO.

BACK CAPE

Put sts that were waiting on waste yarn back onto needle and knit back and forth in St st.

Inc by 1 st using K1f&b on either side of back center st marker on knit side of fabric until cape is wide enough to cover dog's back.

Stop increases, and knit cape to preferred length. BO.

BUTTONS

Put sweater on dog and pull bottom "hammerhead" flap up around belly to determine button placement.

Stitch buttons on WS of sweater.

ADDITIONAL IDEAS

Sew treat pockets on side of cape section or in front to keep your dog motivated on that extralong walk. Place a buttonhole at back neck to accommodate your dog's leash. Knit matching doggie leggings for especially cold days: either knit flat and seam, or knit on appropriately sized DPNs.

JUST LIKE HOME

These patterns could even make base camp on Mount Everest feel like home, bringing both rugged good looks and comfort to your outdoor home-away-from-home. Who knew you could knit a replacement seat for your favorite camp-stool frame? Or that a pillow could do double-duty as both a seat pad and as a sweet-dreams assistant? And everyone needs a cozy blanket to wrap up in—all the better for ghost stories around the campfire.

CAMPFIRE CUSHION

BY SHANNON OKEY

This is a great project for low-light knitting by the campfire; once the initial seed stitch rounds are done, you can knit and knit to your heart's content without worrying about patterns. Of course, if you want to add stitch patterns, this is the perfect blank canvas for any solid, nonlace pattern you like! For the ultimate space-saving camping accessory, leave one edge open. Instead of stuffing with polyfill or a pillow form, put clean T-shirts or other laundry inside when it's time to sleep.

FINISHED SIZE

15" x 10"

MATERIALS

2 skeins of Blue Sky Dyed Cotton from Blue Sky Alpacas (100% organic cotton; 150 yds/137 m; 100 g) in color 603 Thistle

U.S. size 8 (5 mm) circular needle, 16" (41 cm) long

Tapestry needle

16 oz (450 g) of polyfill or appropriately sized pillow form

GAUGE

Not critical

NOTE

Blue Sky also offers naturally colored cotton in several beautiful, muted shades, ranging from palest beige to sage green and even several nutmeglike colors. No bleach or dyes are used in processing.

SPECIAL STITCHES

Seed Stitch

Row 1: *K1, P1*, rep across row.

Row 2: *P1, K1*, rep across row.

Rep rows 1 and 2.

PATTERN

CO 90 sts and join rnd, being careful not to twist sts.

Knit seed st for 10 rnds.

Knit St st until pillow measures 12".

Knit seed st for 10 rnds.

BO.

Turn pillow inside out and sew one end closed with tapestry needle and length of matching yarn. Turn RS out. Stuff with polyfill or insert pillow form, then stitch second side closed. Or, don't stuff it at all and instead use extra clean clothes from your bare-bones camping trip as stuffing.

LACE CAMP STOOL

BY ANNIE MODESITT

Who says campfire seating options have to be boring? With Annie Modesitt's cable-and-lace knitted camp stool, which is considerably stronger than you'd think, you can look hot and stay cool (the airflow that comes through the lace is excellent on a hot summer night). To tell the truth, no one thought this would hold a person's weight either when it arrived at the photo session for the book. So we made Shannon's summer intern, Jodi-Gaye, test it out. She survived, and so did everyone else!

FINISHED SIZE

13" x 19½"

MATERIALS

4 balls of medium-weight sisal twine from
Lehigh (100 yds/91 m) in white (available at
home improvement and hardware stores)

U.S. size 13 (9 mm) needles

Tapestry needle

Cable needle

Camp-stool frame (search thrift and hardware stores for old but sturdy pieces)

GAUGE

5" x 3" over 12 rows of patt (worked in sts
5–17 of chart)

SPECIAL STITCHES

VDD (Vertical Double Decrease): Sl 2 sts as if
to work K2 tog, K1, pass slipped sts over
(dec 2 sts).

C6L (Cable 6 sts with Left twist): Slip 3 sts,
K3, bring slipped sts to front of work and
knit them. (aka C6F: Cable 6 sts to front.)

NOTE

Depending on the size of your camp-stool frame,
you may need to knit your lace piece longer or
shorter or add an extra pattern repeat.

PATTERN

With a double strand of fiber, CO 42 sts.

BEGINNING SUPPORT WRAP

First row: K1, *(YO, K2tog), rep from * to end of row, end K1.

Next row (WS): Purl all sts.

Next row (RS): Knit all sts.

 Rep last 2 rows twice more—6 rows total.

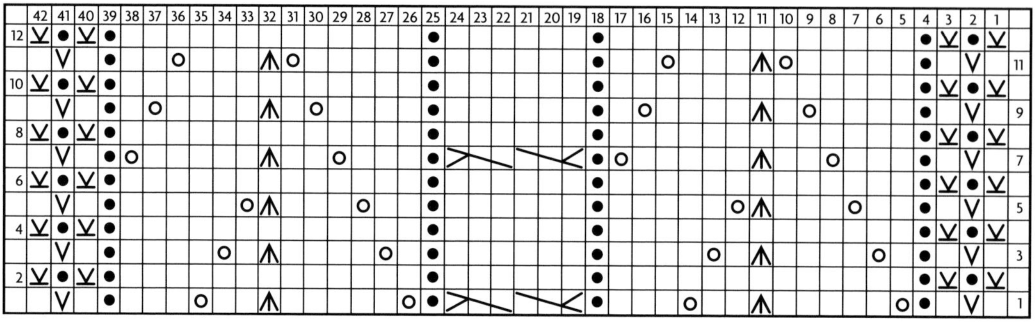

	42	41	40	39	38	37	36	35	34	33	32	31	30	29	28	27	26	25	24	23	22	21	20	19	18	17	16	15	14	13	12	11	10	9	8	7	6	5	4	3	2	1	
12	V	●	V	●														●							●														●	V	●	V	
		V		●			O				Λ	O						●							●		O				Λ	O							●	V			11
10	V	●	V	●														●							●														●	V	●	V	
		V		●		O					Λ		O					●							●	O					Λ		O						●	V			9
8	V	●	V	●														●							●														●	V	●	V	
		V		●	O						Λ			O				●	✕	✕	✕	✕	✕	✕	●	O					Λ			O					●	V			7
6	V	●	V	●														●							●														●	V	●	V	
		V		●				O			Λ				O			●							●			O			Λ				O				●	V			5
4	V	●	V	●														●							●														●	V	●	V	
		V		●					O		Λ					O		●							●				O		Λ					O			●	V			3
2	V	●	V	●														●							●														●	V	●	V	
		V		●					O		Λ						O	●	✕	✕	✕	✕	✕	✕	●				O		Λ						O		●	V			1

(Cells marked ✕ represent the "c3 over 3 left" cable spanning six stitches.)

LEGEND:

Knit
☐
RS: knit stitch
WS: purl stitch

Slip
V
RS: Slip stitch as if to purl, holding yarn in back
WS: Slip stitch as if to purl, holding yarn in front

Purl
●
RS: purl stitch
WS: knit stitch

YO
O
RS: Yarn Over
WS: Yarn Over

Central Double Dec
Λ
RS: Slip first and second stitches together as if to knit. Knit 1 stitch. Pass two slipped stitches over the knit stitch.
WS: Slip first and second stitches together as if to purl through the back loop. Purl 1 stitch. Pass two slipped stitches over the purl stitch.

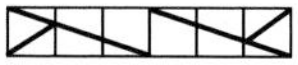

c3 over 3 left
RS: sl3 to CN, hold in front. k3, k3 from CN

Slip wyif
V̲
RS: Slip stitch as if to purl, with yarn in front
WS: Slip stitch as if to purl, with yarn in back

Note: If your stool supports are very wide, you may want to work more than 6 rows.

Next row (WS): K1, *(K2tog, YO), rep from * to end of row, end K1.

BEGIN LACE PATTERN

Next row: Establish lace patt across all sts as foll:

Row 1 (RS): K1, wyif sl 1 (yarn is toward you), K1, *P1, YO, K5, VDD, K2, YO, K3, P1*, C6L, rep from * to *, K1, wyif sl 1, K1.

Row 2 (and all WS rows): wyif sl 1, K1, wyif sl 1, K1, P13, K1, P6, K1, P13, K1, wyif sl 1, K1, wyif sl 1.

Row 3: K1, wyif sl 1, K1, *P1, K1, YO, K4, VDD, K1, YO, K4, P1*, K6, rep from * to *, K1, wyif sl 1, K1.

Row 5: K1, wyif sl 1, K1, *P1, K2, YO, K3, VDD, YO, K5, P1*, K6, rep from * to *, K1, wyif sl 1, K1.

Row 7: K1, wyif sl 1, K1, *P1, K3, YO, K2, VDD, K5, YO, P1*, C6L, rep from * to *, K1, wyif sl 1, K1.

Row 9: K1, wyif sl 1, K1, *P1, K4, YO, K1, VDD, K4, YO, K1, P1*, K6, rep from * to *, K1, wyif sl 1, K1.

Row 11: K1, wyif sl 1, K1, *P1, K5, YO, VDD, K3, YO, K2, P1*, K6, rep from * to *, K1, wyif sl 1, K1.

Row 12: Rep row 2.

Rep these 12 rows until fabric measures 13" (33 cm) from start of lace pattern or desired length between seat supports. End with a WS row.

ENDING SUPPORT WRAP

First row: K1, *(YO, K2tog), rep from * to end of row, end K1.

Next row (WS): Purl all sts.

Next row (RS): Knit all sts.

Rep last 2 rows twice more—6 rows total.

Note: If your stool supports are very wide, you may want to work more than 6 rows.

Next row (WS): K1 *(K2tog, YO), rep from * to end of row, end K1.

BO all sts loosely.

FINISHING

Steam-block piece.

Wrap beginning support-wrap section around one of stool supports. With a single strand of twine and darning needle, "sew" CO edge and next eyelet row, using eyelets as entering and exiting points for darning needle.

Sew bound-off edge to opposite support in the same manner. Sit on your lace camp stool!

SNOWSHOE CAMPING BLANKET

BY JILLIAN MORENO FOR ACME KNITTING CO.

Cuddle up by the fire or in your bed at home with this thick, soft blanket. It's so thick, you could even use it as something to sit on in your tent. The Brown Sheep Burly Spun yarn is extra thick, almost a wool top/pencil-roving weight. If you know someone who spins, you could also substitute pencil roving or even multiple strands of a chunky yarn for the same effect.

FINISHED SIZE

62" x 36"

MATERIALS

MC 6 skeins of Burly Spun yarn from Brown Sheep Company (100% wool; 130 yds) in BS62 Amethyst

CC 4 skeins of Burly Spun yarn in BS300 Mountain Majesty

U.S. size 11 (8 mm) circular needle (see "Note" about length)

Tapestry needle

Cable needle

GAUGE

8 sts and 14 rows = 4"

NOTE

The longer the needle, the better, as this blanket is knit from side to side. Most needles used for knitting blankets or large wraps are 40" (101 cm) or longer.

SPECIAL STITCHES

Seed Stitch

Row 1: *K1, P1*.

Row 2: *P1, K1*.

SNOWSHOE CABLE

C6B: Sl 3 sts to cable needle, hold to back of work, K3, knit 3 sts from cable needle.

C6F: Sl 3 sts to cable needle, hold to front of work, K3, knit 3 sts from cable needle.

PATTERN

CO 12 sts with color MC, 16 sts with color CC, 6 sts with MC, 16 sts with CC, 40 sts with MC, 16 sts with CC, 6 sts with MC, 16 sts with CC, 12 sts with MC.

Keep colors in CO patt throughout blanket, being sure to twist strands when changing color to prevent gaps.

Work 4 rows in seed st.

Beg snowshoe cable patt.

Odd-numbered rows are WS rows; even-numbered rows are RS rows.

Row 1: Work 4 sts in seed st, P8, K2, P12, K2, P6, K2, P12, K2, P40, K2, P12, K2, P6, K2, P12, K2, P8, work 4 sts in seed st.

Row 2: Work 4 sts in seed st, K8, P2, C6B, C6F, P2, K6, P2, C6F, C6B, P2, K40, P2, C6F, C6B, P2, K6, P2, C6B, C6F, P2, K8, work 4 sts in seed st.

Row 3: Rep row 1.

Row 4: Work 4 sts in seed st, K8, P2, K12, P2, K6, P2, K12, P2, K40, P2, K12, P2, K6, P2, K12, P2, K8, work 4 sts in seed st.

Rep rows 3 and 4 until 10 rows have been worked.

Rep the 10 rows 11 more times.

Work 4 rows in seed st.

BO.

FINISHING

Weave in ends.

Pin to size and spritz lightly with water (if you wet-block it, it will take days to dry!); let dry overnight.

CARVER'S HARBOR BLANKET

BY SHANNON OKEY

Reduce, reuse, recycle. Leave only footprints, take only memories. Fans of the outdoors were the original environmentalists, and so I present you with a lap blanket made from either recycled sweaters or leftover bits of yarn. This blanket is named after the main harbor on Vinalhaven, an island off the midcoast of Maine, where the greens and blues and other natural colors fade together into a glorious swirl that changes from hour to hour all day. You can use colors that reflect your favorite camping spot or outdoor location, from rusts and browns inspired by a redwood forest to the many shades of gray and green on a lichen-covered rock face.

FINISHED SIZE

Varies depending on your preference and size of chosen rotary-cut squares

MATERIALS

4 (or more!) old sweaters and/or feltable
    wool yarns from your stash

Sewing machine or a sewing needle

Coordinating thread

6" (15 cm) square plastic quilting grid

Rotary cutter

Steam iron

Plastic hairbrush (optional)

Sharp scissors

Straight pins

GAUGE

Not critical

NOTE

If you have a large supply of feltable wool yarns, no matter how small the amounts, you can also knit squares to make this blanket, and either felt them before assembly or not. If you choose to felt them, you will need to knit them larger than 6" (15 cm) square and slightly longer than they are wide. The structure of knitted felt is such that it loses much more length than width as it shrinks.

PATTERN

If using sweaters:

> Wash your sweaters with a hot wash and cold rinse to shrink them.

> Cut sweaters open at the seams and iron pieces as flat as possible.

If using either sweaters or felted squares:

Lightly iron felted squares.

Cut out as many squares from each sweater as you can, and/or use the quilting grid to trim up the edges of the felted squares.

ASSEMBLY

On a large, flat surface (beds are good for this!) arrange your squares in desired pattern. The more colors and textures, the better!

Pin squares tog in strips and sew individual squares tog using a straight st.

Sew strips tog.

FINISHING

Re-iron finished blanket and trim off excess threads. If any felted pieces have large chunks of lint or felted bits on the surface, brush them off firmly using a hairbrush.

CARE INSTRUCTIONS

Wash in cold water, hang to dry, and refresh with steam iron when fully or mostly dry.

HEAD TO TOE

Mom was right: a quality hat will keep you warmer than almost any piece of clothing! Here are patterns for two hats, two pairs of socks, and a pair of mittens; wear them in the woods or in town—either way, you'll never be chilly again!

COUGAR MOUNTAIN SOCKS

BY ARIEL ALTARAS

These socks are great if your feet tend to get hot in your boots. The combination of lovely, padded wool and heat-wicking bamboo make for a great pair—of fibers *and* socks!—on the hiking trail. Although these were originally meant for men, their subtle beauty looks great on women, too.

SIZE

Men's or larger Women's

MATERIALS

1 ball of Trekking Pro Natura from Skacel
(75% wool, 25% bamboo; 420 m; 100 g) in
color 1602

Set of U.S. size 1 (2.25 mm) double-pointed
needles

Tapestry needle

GAUGE

8½ sts = 1" (2.5 cm)

PATTERN

CO 80 sts.

Knit cuff in ribbing as foll: *K1, P1, K2, P1, K2, P1, K1, P1, rep from * to end of round.

Rnds 1–16: Knit ribbing (cuff measures approximately 1½" (4 cm).

Rnd 17: Knit.

Rnd 18: Purl.

Rnds 19 and 20: Knit.

Beg mountain chart.

Rep around (8 reps), then work as foll:

Rnd 1: Knit.

Rnd 2: Purl.

Rnd 3: Knit.

Rnd 4: Knit.

On next row, beg working in ribbing as before: *K1, P1, K2, P1, K2, P1, K1, P1, rep from * to end of rnd. Cont in ribbing until cuff measures 8" (20 cm) or desired length.

On next rnd of ribbing, position sts for instep and heel flap: instep should have 37 sts, beg with P1, K2 and ending with K2, P1. Rem 43 sts will form heel flap.

HEEL FLAP

First row: Sl 1, K2tog, *sl 1, K1*, rep from * to * across. Turn, sl 1, and purl across.

Rep foll 2 rows until there are 20 slipped sts on each side of heel flap:

Row 1: *Sl 1, K1*, rep from * to * across.

Row 2: Sl 1, purl across.

HEEL TURN

Row 1: Sl 1, K23, SSK, K1, turn.

Row 2: Sl 1, P7, P2tog, P1, turn.

Row 3: Sl 1, knit to 1 st before gap, SSK, K1, turn.

Row 4: Sl 1, purl to 1 st before gap, P2tog, P1, turn.

Rep rows 3 and 4 until all sts are worked, ending with row 4. Knit across rem 24 sts, placing a marker in center, and pick up 20 gusset sts. Knit in established rib patt across instep stitches and pick up 21 sts on other side of gusset.

Dec gusset stitches until 37 sts rem as foll:

Front: Cont in established patt.

Back: Knit 2 rnds as foll:

Rnd 1: K1, SSK, knit to last 3 sts, K2tog, K1.

Rnd 2: Knit.

	10	9	8	7	6	5	4	3	2	1	
10											
											9
8											
	●					●			●		7
6	●	●				●	●		●	●	
	●	●			●	●	●	●	●	●	5
4	●	●	●		●	●	●	●	●	●	
	●	●	●	●	●	●	●	●	●	●	3
2	●	●	●	●	●	●	●	●	●	●	
	●	●	●	●	●	●	●	●	●	●	1

LEGEND:

● **Purl**
RS: purl stitch

☐ **Knit**
RS: knit stitch

After dec to 32 sole sts, cont knitting instep sts in patt while knitting sole sts every row. Remove marker. When foot measures approximately 2" less than desired final length, end after finishing instep sts. Rnd now starts at sole sts. Beg toe shaping as foll:

Rnd 1: Knit.

Rnd 2: K1, SSK, knit to last 3 sole sts, K2tog, K1. On instep sts K1, SSK, knit to last 3 instep sts, K2tog, K1.

Work these 2 rnds 8 times (42 total sts), then work rnd 2 every rnd until 22 sts rem. Graft sts tog and weave in ends.

TWISTS AND TURNS SOCKS

BY ARIEL ALTARAS

These stylish cabled socks are sure to turn heads. You'll love their sleek fit and how fast they knit up! No matter what color yarn you use, Twists and Turns looks stunning and will keep you comfy all day long in even the toughest conditions.

SIZE

Women's Medium

MATERIALS

1 skein of Socks that Rock Lightweight from Blue Moon Fiber Arts (100% superwash merino wool; 360 yds; 4.5 oz) in Jade

Set of U.S. size 1 (2.5 mm) double-pointed needles

GAUGE

7½ sts = 1" (2.5 cm)

SPECIAL STITCHES

RT (Right Twist): Knit 2 sts tog, but leave sts on needle, then knit first st and pull both sts off left needle.

LT (Left Twist): Knit second st on left needle tbl and leave st on needle, then knit first 2 sts tog tbl and pull both sts off left needle.

C4L (Cable 4 Left): Slip 2 sts to cable needle and hold in front, K2, knit 2 sts from cable needle.

C4R (Cable 4 Right): Sl 2 sts to cable needle and hold in back, K2, knit 2 sts from cable needle.

PATTERN

CO 64 sts and join in the rnd, being careful not to twist sts.

RIBBING

Front needle(s): P1, K4, P2, *K2, P2* 5 times, K4, P1.

Back needle(s): K2, P2, K2, P1, K4, P1, K3, P2, K3, P1, K4, P1, K2, P2, K2.

Cont in established ribbing for 10 rnds, then beg leg patt.

LEG

Rnds 1 and 3

Front: P1, K4, P1, K20, P1, K4, P1.

Back: K6, P1, K4, P1, K3, P2, K3, P1, K4, P1, K6.

Rnd 2

Front: P1, K4, P1, K20, P1, K4, P1.

Back: RT 3 times, P1, K4, P1, K3, P2, K3, P1, K4, P1, LT 3 times.

Rnd 4

Front: P1, C4R, P1, K20, P1, C4L, P1.

Back: K1, RT 2 times, K1, P1, C4R, P1, K3, P2, K3, P1, C4L, P1, K1, LT 2 times, K1.

Knit leg patt for about 15 reps, until sock measures 7" (18 cm) or desired length. Beg next rep and end after working rnd 3 on front (instep) sts only.

HEEL FLAP

Heel flap is worked across back needle.

Row 1: *Sl 1, K1* across row.

Row 2: Sl 1, purl across row.

Rep these 2 rows 16 times—17 chain sts on edge of heel flap.

HEEL TURN

Row 1: Sl 1, K18, SSK, K1, turn.

Row 2: Sl 1, P7, P2tog, P1, turn.

Row 3: Sl 1, knit to 1 st before gap, SSK, K1, turn.

Row 4: Sl 1, purl to 1 st before gap, P2tog, P1, turn.

Rep rows 3 and 4 until all stitches have been worked—20 sts rem. Knit across and pick up 17 gusset sts, knit in established patt (rnd 4) across front (instep), and pick up 17 sts on other side of gusset.

Dec gusset sts until 32 sts rem as foll:

Front: Cont in established patt.

Back: Knit 2 rnds as foll:

Rnd 1: K1, SSK, knit to last 3 sts, K2tog, K1.

Rnd 2: Knit.

After dec to 32 sole sts, cont knitting front (instep) sts in patt while knitting back (sole) sts every row. When foot measures 7½" (19 cm) or 2" (5 cm) less than desired length, beg toe shaping as foll:

Row 1: On instep needle(s), K1, SSK, knit to last 3 sts K2tog, K1; on sole needle(s), K1, SSK, knit to last 3 sts, K2tog, K1.

Row 2: Knit.

Rep these 2 rows 6 times (36 total sts rem), then work row 1 another 4 times—20 total sts rem. Cut yarn and graft stitches to close toe.

ALMOST AUTUMN HAT

BY SHANNON OKEY

I love the time of year when the leaves are just beginning to turn. Even on the same tree, some turn yellow while others remain green. This hat incorporates many interesting details, including post-felting ribbing and a crown shaped with simple sewn stitches to add to its visual effect.

SIZE

One size fits most adults; bottom edge stretched is approximately 20" (50 cm).

MATERIALS

MC 1 skein of Cascade 220 from Cascade Yarns (100% wool, 220 yds) in color 4010

CC 1 skein of Cascade 220 in color 2452

Cotton waste yarn

U.S. size 8 (5 mm) circular needle, 16" (41 cm) long

Set of 4 U.S. size 8 (5 mm) double-pointed needles

Tapestry needle

Sewing needle and coordinating thread

Straight pins

GAUGE

16 sts and 22 rows = 4" (10 cm) before felting, but exact gauge is not critical

NOTE

This hat is a little on the large side, but the knit ribbing (added to the hat after felting) will generally pull it in tight enough for most adult heads. If you're knitting this for a younger person or someone with a smaller-than-average head, you may want to cast on 80 or 85 stitches instead of 90.

PATTERN

Provisionally CO 90 sts with CC and cotton waste yarn.

Join rnd, being careful not to twist sts, and knit 22 rnds.

Changing to MC, knit another 24 rnds.

Beg dec rnds (when things get tight on your needle, switch to DPNs):
K2tog tbl, K1 around—45 sts.
Knit 4 rnds.
K2tog tbl, K1 around—30 sts.
Knit 3 rnds.
K2tog tbl, K1 around—15 sts.
Knit 2 rnds.

Cut yarn, leaving 12" tail, and using tapestry needle, slip remaining sts onto yarn. Pull closed and weave in ends.

If your gauge is very tight and you cannot easily close rem gap, you may need to knit another round or two, possibly even a fourth dec rnd. Keep in mind the hat will shrink when felted, so a small gap is not a big deal.

FELTING

Felt hat by running through hot wash/cold rinse cycle in your washing machine. Depending on your local water and machine, this may take two cycles. If you are making this for a smaller head, such as a child's, definitely do two cycles.

Place hat on coffee can or something similar to dry.

FINISHING

Turn hat WS out and pinch an inch between your fingers and the crown (where dec rnds beg). Pin all around hat with straight pins. Using a sewing needle and thread, stitch around crown with small running stitches (a straight line of dashes) and fasten off. Turn hat RS out. This forms the disc and shaped-crown effect. Without the excess felt tucked away to the inside to shape the crown, this hat would most likely cover your eyes! If you prefer, you can also stitch this RS out using a sharp-tipped tapestry needle and short sts with CC yarn.

Remove cotton waste yarn from provisional CO and return sts to circular needle. Knit another 10 rnds of CC 1 x 1 rib (*K1, P1* around) to finish hat.

VERMONT LEAVES HAT

BY SHANNON OKEY

This is a great hat for active outdoorspeople. The cable crossings form small, protected natural vents to get rid of excess heat while you're running or chopping firewood. Its close-fitting shape looks good on everyone, and it's an excellent first-time cable project.

SIZE

One size fits most adults; finished edge is approximately 20" (50 cm) unstretched.

MATERIALS

1 skein of O-Wool Classic from Vermont Organic Fiber Company (100% organic merino wool; 198 yds) in color Sumac

U.S. size 8 (5 mm) circular needle, 16" (41 cm) long

Set of 4 U.S. size 8 (5 mm) double-pointed needles

Tapestry needle

Single double-pointed needle or cable needle

GAUGE

Approximately 4 sts = 1" (2.5 cm) in St st

SPECIAL STITCHES

C6F: Cable 3 sts over 3 sts, with held sts to front.

NOTE

If you've never made a cable stitch before, it's simple! Just think about it this way: you're placing stitches onto a spare needle so you can knit them out of order. In the case of the cable used here, instead of knitting your stitches 1-2-3-4-5-6, you're slipping 1-2-3 to your DPN or cable needle, then holding them at the front of the work while you knit 4-5-6. After 4-5-6 are knitted, you then knit 1-2-3. So, 1-2-3-4-5-6 becomes 4-5-6-1-2-3!

PATTERN

CO 78 sts and join, being careful not to twist sts.

K3, P3 around for 8 rnds.

K3, K1f&b, P2 around—91 sts.

Knit 5 rnds.

C6F, K1, rep around.

Knit 5 rnds.

C6F, K1, rep around.

Knit 9 rnds.

BEGIN DECREASE ROUNDS

Rnd 1: *K2tog, K9* around to last 5 sts, K5.

Rnd 2: Knit.

Rnd 3: *K2tog, K8* around to last 3 sts, K3.

Rnd 4: Knit.

Rnd 5: *K2tog, K7* around to last st, K1.

Rnd 6: Knit.

Rnd 7: *K2tog, K6* around to last 2 sts, K2.

Rnd 8: Knit.

Rnd 9: *K2tog, K5* around to last 2 sts, K2.

Rnd 10: Knit.

Rnd 11: *K2tog, K4* around to last st, K1.

Rnd 12: Knit.

Rnd 13: *K2tog, K3* around.

Rnd 14: Knit.

Rnd 15: *K2tog, K2* until 21 sts rem.
Cut yarn, leaving 12" tail. Slip sts
to tapestry needle, pull closed, and
weave in ends.

FINISHING

This hat really looks better after a wet block.
Completely immerse hat in cool water,
shake out excess, then dry on Styrofoam
head form (my personal choice; they cost
a few dollars at a wig or a costume-supply
shop but really come in handy if you like
to make hats), or stuff with plastic grocery
bags and place on top of a coffee can or
something similar.

LAKE EFFECT DOUBLE-KNIT MITTENS

BY ALISON TAYLOR

These mittens are great made in sets. One skein of Cascade EcoWool alone will make several pairs, but switch up the color of the lining and contrasting color work to keep track of which pair is which!

SIZE

Women's Small/Medium (Women's Large/
Men's Small to Medium; Child's
Medium/Large)

MATERIALS

MC 1 skein of EcoWool from Cascade Yarns
(100% wool; 478 yds; 250 g) in color 8095
Exterior

CC 1 skein of Indulgence from Cascade Yarns
(70% alpaca, 30% angora; 123 yds; 50 g) in
white

Sets of 5 U.S. sizes 8 and 9 double-pointed
needles

Cotton waste yarn

Cable needle or spare double-pointed
needle

Tapestry needle

GAUGE

Not critical

NOTES

Double knitting is a great way to simultaneously create a lining that has the same gauge and dimensions of the original work. Essentially, each row has two rounds: one for the outer color where the main color is in stockinette and the other for the liner in reverse stockinette. The color work in this mitten secures the lining to the mitten body without a need for any sewing. The Fair Isle work is achieved by slipping stitches and pulling the CC through to the outside. You must keep the slipped stitches close together or the MC will "puff out" from the CC border. A little puff gives your work some texture, but too much will just look like a haphazard loose gauge.

You can use either the chart or the written directions for the color, but keep in mind that the liner stitches have been omitted. None of the liner stitches are done in MC so if you see any MC on the inside, you have made an error in your slipping. It will become easier as you go along; just remember that liner stitches should be slipped with the yarn held to the front and mitten stitches should be slipped with the yarn to the back.

The stitch counts refer to the number of *each* stitch unless noted. Sizing is approximate. Not everyone has long palms with medium fingers and a fat thumb like I do. Feel free to reduce or increase by multiples of two stitches as needed. You might want a longer cuff to keep snow out of your kid's wrist or a looser one (use the larger needles throughout) for that man who hates anything clingy.

Over time, these mittens will felt natural-ly and become more watertight. The angora in the liner makes them very soft but also quite warm. If you substitute yarns, do not put acrylic or cotton in the liner: it will stay wet and cold longer than natural fibers. A nylon blend is better if you must substitute.

PATTERN

CUFF

With smaller needles, CO 24 (28, 20) sts of MC on needle 1. CO 24 (28, 20) sts of CC on needle 2.

Holding CC in *front*, sl 8 (9, 6) sts of each color onto needle 3, beg with MC and alternating 8 (10, 8) sts on needle 4 and 8 (9, 6) sts on needle 5.

Beg with needle 5 so that CC is on the outside and join begins on row 2, work foll rows:

Row 1: With MC: *K1, YF, slp, P1, slp, YB* around. With CC: *slp, YF, P1, YB, slp, K1* around.

Rows 2–12: Rep row 1.

BODY

Switch to larger needles and work foll rows:

Row 1: With MC: *K1, YF, slp, YB* around, inc in sts 1, 7, 13, 19 (1, 8, 15, 22; 1, 6, 11, 16) by K1f&b 28 (32, 24).

With CC: *Slp, YF, P1, YB* around, inc *between* each set of 2 MC sts by picking up from row below.

Row 2: With CC: *K1, P1* around.

	8	7	6	5	4	3	2	1	
10	■	■	■	■	■	■	■	■	
	■		■				■		9
8	■		■		■		■		
		■		■		■		■	7
6	■		■		■		■		
	■		■		■		■		5
4		■		■		■		■	
	■		■		■		■		3
2	■		■		■		■		
	■	■	■	■	■	■	■	■	1

LEGEND:

■ CC   □ MC

	8	7	6	5	4	3	2	1	
4	■	■	■	■	■	■	■	■	
	■		■		■		■		3
2	■		■		■		■		
	■	■	■	■	■	■	■	■	1

LEGEND:

■ CC   □ MC

Row 3: With MC: *K1, YF, slp, YB* around. With CC: *slp, YF, P1, YB* around.

Row 3 establishes St st patt.

THUMB GUSSET

Even rows are worked plain.

Row 1: Maintaining St st, K1f&b in MC sts 1 and 4, picking up from row below in CC.

Row 3: K1f&b in sts 1 and 6.

Row 5 (Adult sizes only): K1f&b in sts 1 and 8

Row 7 (Adult Large only): K1f&b in sts 1 and 10

There should be 34 (40, 28) sts on your needles.

Rows 9 and 10: Work St st even.

Row 11: Using waste yarn, [K1, P1] 10 (12, 8) sts of each color. Sl sts back onto needle and reestablish St st patt.

Row 12: Knit.

Row 13: On first 2 and last 2 sts, rearranging as necessary with spare needle, K2tog—32 (38, 26) sts.

COLOR WORK (SEE CHART 1)

Row 1: With CC, *K1, P1* around.

Row 2: With MC, *K1, YF, slp, YB, slp, YF, slp, YB* around. With CC, *slp, YF, P1, K1, P1, YB* around.

Row 3: Rep row 2.

Row 4: With MC, *slp, YF, slp, YB, K1, YF, slp, YB* around. With CC, *K1, P1, YB, slp, YF, P1* around.

Rows 5 and 6: Rep row 2.

Row 7: Rep row 4.

Rows 8 and 9: Rep row 2.

Row 10: Rep row 1.

Returning to St st and solid colors, knit 12 (16, 8) rows *or adjust* to fit length.

DECREASE ROW

Using a spare needle to rearrange sts, K2tog evenly around to reduce by 4 (5, 3) sts—28 (33, 23) sts. P2tog on CC round.

Work 1 row even.

Using a spare needle to rearrange stitches, K2tog evenly around to reduce by 4 (5, 3) sts—24 (28, 20 sts. P2tog on CC rnd.

Work 1 row even.

Cont until there are 16 (18, 14) sts each of MC and CC rem.

With MC, K2tog, joining MC and CC sts.

Rearrange sts so there are 8 (9, 7) on 2 needles.

Turn mitten inside out and use three-needle bind off to finish.

THUMB

Carefully removing sts from waste yarn, use MC and CC to reestablish St st from *both sides* of waste yarn and arrange sts evenly on 4 needles [20 (24, 16) of each color]. Using 4 needles makes it easier to work on a small number of sts, but you can use 3 if it is easier for you.

Rows 1 and 2: Work even.

Row 3: On sts 1 and 11 (13, 9), rearranging as necessary with spare needle, K2tog 18 (22, 14) sts, P2tog with CC.

Row 4: Knit.

Row 5: On sts 1 and 10 (12, 8) K2tog—16 (20, 12) sts.

THUMB COLOR WORK (SEE CHART 2)

Rows 1–3: Work as for main color work.

Row 4: With CC, *K1, P1* around.

Returning to St st in solid color, work even for 4 (8, 2) rows or to desired length.

*On next row 2, rearranging as needed, K2tog/P2tog 4 (5, 3) times evenly around.

Work 1 row even twice [8 (10, 6) of each color].

With MC, K2tog, joining MC and CC 8 (10, 6).

Using a tapestry needle, pull MC through all stitches and secure.

Weave in ends. At join of cuff, secure row 1 with MC and use CC to create a st across join to make CC edge continuous.

Rep for second mitten.

STAYING CLEAN AND COMFORTABLE

When you're a long way from the nearest port-a-potty, let alone bathroom, staying clean and comfortable becomes a priority. This chapter features washcloths, towels, and other items that will help you keep both yourself and the campsite tidy.

WOODSY WASHCLOTH

BY AMY POLCYN

Save those soap slivers! Once they're too small to be used in your bathroom, slip them into the inner pocket of this nifty washcloth and get every last bit of use from them. If you're venturing into the deep woods, check your local health-food or camp-outfitting store for soaps that resist bugs. There are several types of herbal soaps that will make you taste horrible to biting insects. You'll want to make several of these excellent, environmentally responsible dishcloths, which you can machine wash (instead of buying new sponges constantly). They may full a little bit over time due to the wool content, but will hold up to even the toughest scrubbing!

FINISHED SIZE

8" x 8" (20 cm x 20 cm)

MATERIALS

1 skein of HempWol 4 from Lanaknits Designs Hemp for Knitting (50% hemp, 50% wool; 254 yds/240 m; 100 g) in color 10 Peridot

U.S. size 6 (4 mm) straight needles or size needed to obtain gauge, 14" (36 cm) long

Tapestry needle

GAUGE

20 sts and 28 rows = 4" (10 cm) in patt st

SPECIAL STITCHES

Seed Stitch

Row 1: *K1, P1*.

Row 2: *P1, K1*.

NOTES

This washcloth will full slightly with use; however, the yarn does not felt well, so size should not change appreciably. If you want to tie this to a tree for drip-drying purposes, attach an I-cord or simply thread a piece of yarn through the corner of the washcloth with a tapestry needle and drip away! See the Camp Towel instructions for details.

PATTERN

WASHCLOTH FRONT

CO 42 sts.

Rows 1, 3, 5 (WS): P2, *[K1f&b] twice, P2, rep from * to end of row.

Rows 2, 4, 6: K2, *[P2tog] twice, K2, rep from * to end of row.

Rows 7, 9, 11: [K1f&b] twice, *P2, [K1f&b] twice, rep from * to end of row.

Rows 8, 10, 12: [P2tog] twice, *K2, [P2tog] twice, rep from * to end of row.

Rep rows 1–12 until piece measures 8" from beg. BO.

WASHCLOTH BACK (MAKE 2)

CO 42 sts.

Work in St st for 5" (13 cm). Work 1" (2.5 cm) more in seed st. BO.

FINISHING

With RS facing, overlap back pieces on front, with seed-st strips toward center. Position back pieces so lower back piece has knit side facing and upper back piece has purl side facing. Whipstitch sides and weave in ends. Turn washcloth to RS and slip a favorite bar of soap inside.

CAMP TOWEL

BY AMY POLCYN

Keeping things clean can be a challenge, and so is finding a towel rack in the wilderness! No worries with this towel, though. You can get it wet and scrub whatever you like, then tie it with the attached cords to the nearest low-hanging tree branch to drip-dry. Its open-weave pattern helps it dry even faster!

FINISHED SIZE

12" x 17" (30 cm x 43 cm)

MATERIALS

2 skeins of Allhemp 6 from Lanaknits Designs Hemp for Knitting (100% long-fiber hemp; 165 yds/150 m; 100 g) in color 021 Dijon

U.S. size 6 (4 mm) straight needles or size needed to obtain gauge, 14" (36 cm) long

Lucet tool or 2 U.S. size 4 (3.5 mm) double-pointed needles

Cable needle

Tapestry needle

GAUGE

20 sts and 26 rows = 4" using larger needles in patt st

SPECIAL STITCHES

Right purl twist: Slip next purl st to cable needle, hold to back. Knit next st, purl st from cable needle.

Left purl twist: Slip next knit st to cable needle, hold to front. Purl next st, knit st from cable needle.

SEED STITCH

Row 1: *K1, P1*.

Row 2: *P1, K1*.

PATTERN

With larger needles, CO 60 sts. Work in seed st for 1" (2.5 cm), ending with a RS row.

Next row (WS): Work 5 sts in seed st, K1, *K3, P2, K3; rep from * to last 6 sts, K1, work last 5 sts in seed st.

Next row: Work 5 sts in seed st, work row 1 of patt chart across next 50 sts, finish row in seed st.

Cont as established, foll chart over center 50 sts and working first and last 5 sts in seed st throughout, until piece measures 16" (41 cm), ending with row 4 of chart. Work 1 more inch in seed st. BO.

TIES

Using Lucet tool or DPNs, make Lucet cord (following package instructions) or make a 3-st I-cord for 28" (71 cm). Fasten off.

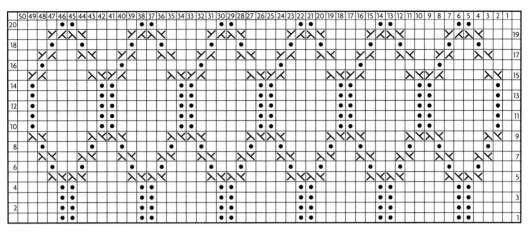

LEGEND:

Knit
☐ RS: knit stitch
WS: purl stitch

Purl
⊡ RS: purl stitch
WS: knit stitch

Left Twist
RS: sl1 to CN, hold in front. k1, k1 from CN
WS: Left Twist

Right Twist
RS: Skip the first stitch, knit into 2nd stitch, then knit skipped stitch. Slip both stitches from needle together OR k2tog leaving sts on LH needle, then k first st again. sl both sts off needle.
WS: Skip first stitch, and purl the 2nd stitch, then purl the skipped stitch. Slip both sts from needle together.

FINISHING

Weave in ends. Fold cord in half, insert folded end through upper right corner of towel (between sts), pull ends through loop, and tighten. Tie ends of cord in overhand knots. Block lightly.

CLOUDWALKER PADDED SHOE INSERTS

BY AMY GUMM

Sensitive feet? Hiking boots getting a bit worn? Knit yourself some cushy, padded shoe inserts and forget the flimsy drugstore kind. These inserts, knitted from machine-washable merino wool, can be washed and refreshed indefinitely, unlike others.

SIZE

Women's Small (Women's Medium/Men's Small, Women's Large/Men's Medium, Men's Large)

MATERIALS

1 skein of Gems Sport Weight from Louet (100% merino wool; 225 yds; 100 g) in color 42 Eggplant

U.S. size 3 (3.25 mm) needle

GAUGE

26 sts and 52 rows = 4" (10 cm)

SPECIAL STITCHES

Kb&f: Knit into back and front of st (similar, but not the same, as K1f&b).

PATTERN

CO 6 (7, 7, 8) sts.

Row 1: K1, Kb&f, K2 (3, 3, 4), Kb&f, K1.

Row 2: K1, Kb&f, K4 (5, 5, 7), Kb&f, K1.

Row 3: K1, Kb&f, K6 (7, 7, 8), Kb&f, K1.

Row 4: K1, Kb&f, K8 (9, 9, 10), Kb&f, K1.

Row 5: Knit.

Row 6: K1, Kb&f, K10 (11, 11, 12), Kb&f, K1.

Rows 7–9: Knit.

Row 10: K14 (15, 15, 16), Kb&f, K1.

Rows 11–13: Knit.

Row 14: K1, Kb&f, K15 (16, 16, 17).

Rows 15–34 (38, 40, 44): Knit.

Row 35 (39, 41, 45): K1, Kb&f, K12 (13, 13, 14), Kb&f, K1.

Rows 36 (40, 42, 46)–59 (63, 65, 69): Knit.

Row 60 (64, 66, 70): Knit to last 2 sts, Kb&f, K1.

Rows 61 (65, 67, 71)–70 (74, 76, 80): Knit.

Row 71 (75, 77, 81): K1, Kb&f, knit to last 2 sts, Kb&f, K1.

Rows 72 (76, 78, 82)–78 (82, 84, 88): Knit.

Row 79 (83, 85, 89): Knit to last 2 sts, Kb&f, K1.

Rows 80 (84, 86, 90)–86 (90, 92, 96): Knit.

Row 87 (91, 93, 97): Knit to last 2 sts, Kb&f, K1.

Rows 88 (92, 94, 98)–98 (102, 104, 108): Knit.

Row 99 (103, 105, 109): K1, K2tog, knit to end of row.

Rows 100 (104, 106, 110)–113 (117, 119, 123): Knit.

Row 114 (118, 120, 124): K1, K2tog, knit to last 3 sts, K2tog, K1.

Rows 115 (119, 121, 125)–120 (124, 126, 130): Knit.

Row 121 (125, 127, 131): K1, K2tog, knit to end of row.

Rows 122 (126, 128, 132)–123 (127, 129, 133): Knit.

Row 124 (128, 130, 134): K1, K2tog, knit to last 3 sts, K2tog, K1.

Row 125 (129, 131, 135): Knit.

Row 126 (130, 132, 136): K1, K2tog, knit to last 3 sts, K2tog, K1.

Rows 127 (131, 133, 137)–130 (134, 136, 140): Knit.

Row 131 (135, 137, 141): K1, K2tog, knit to end of row.

Row 132 (136, 138, 142): K1, K2tog, knit to last 3 sts, K2tog, K1.

Row 133 (137, 139, 141): K1, K2tog, knit to end of row.

Row 134 (138, 140, 142): K1, K2tog, knit to last 3 sts, K2tog, K1.

Row 135 (139, 141, 145): K1, K2tog, knit to last 3 sts, K2tog, K1.

Row 136 (140, 142, 146): K1, K2tog, knit to last 3 sts, K2tog, K1.

FINISHING

Weave in ends. Put in your shoes!

Hint: If you like extra cushioning or have sensitive feet, knit 2 per shoe and stitch them together for more padding.

AL FRESCO DINING

Whether you're going on a picnic or a four-day trek through the woods, it's important to dine in style. Use Minnie Olson's knit hammock to keep bears and ants (or maybe just hungry teenagers!) out of your cooler. Keep silverware from bouncing around your pack with a stylish cutlery roll that doubles as a place mat—it makes even granola bars seem appetizing—and wash it all down with fresh, cold water from your Ell Pond Nalgene cozy. Need something sweet after dinner? We've got you covered with combo marshmallow-stick holders/potholders, perfect for making s'mores.

COOLER HAMMOCK

BY MINNIE OLSON

Transform plain cotton household twine into a handy tool you can use both at home and away. This cooler hammock is great both at the campground and in the backyard. If you can't find heavy cotton twine at your local hardware store or don't like the substitute yarn choices, you could also use nylon twine.

FINISHED SIZE

Fits six-pack-sized Igloo-style cooler.

MATERIALS

2 balls of medium-weight cotton household twine (140 yds/128 m), available at hardware stores

Suggested substitute yarns: Lion Brand Kitchen Cotton, Peaches & Cream, or any worsted-weight unmercerized cotton

2 washers, 2½" (6 cm) diameter, with large center hole

U.S. size 7 (4.5 mm) straight or circular needles (metal works better with cotton) or size needed to obtain gauge

U.S. size 7 (4.5mm) double-pointed needles or same size as other needles

Tapestry needle

GAUGE

20 sts = 4½" (11 cm) in St st before washing

20 rows = 3½ 2" (9 cm) in St st before washing

20 sts = 3¾" (9.5 cm) in St st after washing

20 rows = 2" (5 cm) in St st after washing

Be sure to knit a swatch to determine your gauge (see "Note" below). You're after a fairly firm fabric with the ribbing, but the mesh can be fairly open.

NOTE

Mercerized cotton, also known as pearl or pearle cotton, has been treated with a caustic soda bath and then neutralized in a mild acid bath to increase its strength and decrease lint. Unmercerized cotton, as used in this pattern, will shrink, so it's very important to knit a swatch and wash it before you start. If you do choose to use mercerized cotton, keep this in mind and swatch accordingly.

PATTERN 1

Row 1: *K1, K2tog*, rep across row, end K1.

Rows 2 and 4: Purl.

Row 3: *K2tog, K1*, rep across row, end K2tog.

CO 37 sts and knit 1 x 1 rib for 11" (28 cm).

BO all sts, but do not fasten off. Turn work and pick up 36 sts in back loops of BO, creating a ridge.

Work in patt 1 for 9" (23 cm). Beg dec until 3 sts rem.

DECREASING FOR PATTERN 1

Work rows 1 and 3 as written. On WS, P1, P2tog tbl, purl to last 3 sts, P2tog tbl, P1.

Switch to DPNs. Knit I-cord for 48" (122 cm). Do not BO. Take washer and sl the 3 sts through hole. Sew live sts to I-cord, creating a loop.

PATTERN 2

Row 1: *P1, P2tog tbl*, rep across row, end P1.

Rows 2 and 4: Knit.

Row 3: *P2tog tbl, P1*, rep across row, end P2tog tbl.

On CO edge, pick up 37 sts in bars of first row, creating a ridge similar to one on other end.

Work in patt 2 for 9" (23 cm). Beg dec until 3 sts rem.

DECREASING FOR PATTERN 2

Work rows 1 and 3 as written. On WS, K1, K2tog, knit to last 3 sts, K2tog, K1.

Work second I-cord same as first, attaching washer at end.

SIDE STRAPS

Lay hammock on table and hold up lace panels to form a U. On RS, measure 6" (16 cm) up right mesh panel and pick up 6 sts. Work in garter st (knit every row) for 6" (16 cm), then attach to left-hand mesh panel in same place so strap is horizontal. The designer used whipstitch, but mattress stitch will also work well if you prefer. Turn hammock around and rep on second side.

FINISHING

Weave in all ends but do not clip tails. Wash hammock in your washing machine using warm water, which will cause shrinking. After washing, block it by putting it on the cooler. Allow to dry, then clip tails. Waiting until the cotton is washed and dried before clipping the tails causes them to stay where you want them.

Fill cooler, then toss the washers attached to the I-cord over a sturdy branch, one from either side. Tie off with a loose knot.

SUPERFLUFF MARSHMALLOW-STICK HOLDERS

BY SHANNON OKEY

These are excellent small projects for impatient knitters: the perfect blank canvas for trying out new stitches or techniques, using up gauge swatches you didn't bother to pull out, or getting rid of stash yarn (as long as it's wool).

FINISHED SIZE

6" x 6" (15 cm x 15 cm) or whatever size you like (see "Note")

MATERIALS

1 skein of Cascade 220 from Cascade Yarns (100% wool; 220 yds) in color 7825

Tapestry needle

Cotton (not poly-blend) batting (optional)

U.S. size 8 (5 mm) needles

GAUGE

Not critical

NOTE

Why should you only use wool yarn for these? Wool is fire-resistant, and if you choose to insert an extra layer of cotton batting between the two sides, they'll even be tough enough to take hot pans off the campfire. Why cotton and not polyester-blend batting? The thicker the better, and also some poly blends may melt or catch fire when exposed to extreme heat.

PATTERN

CO 30 sts or number of sts required to make a piece 6" (15 cm) wide.

Knit in St st or garter st (knit every row) until piece measures 6" (15 cm) long, then purl on a knit row to form a clear fold line.

Knit an additional 6" (15 cm) and BO.

Stitch sides together with tapestry needle and piece of matching yarn, inserting cotton batting, if desired, before sewing final side closed.

FINISHING

These look really great with some very elementary quilting if you stuff them with batting. Just run a line of stitches along the outer border and diagonally through the middle. You can even put your initial in the middle so no one will steal your perfectly crisped marshmallow!

ELL POND NALGENE COZY

BY SHANNON OKEY

Ell Pond is a beautiful, large pond near my aunt's house in southern Maine. My aunt swims there every day she can, as its clear water and bottom covered with pleasantly squishy leaves are truly something to look forward to on a hot summer day. With a lovely bottle cozy like this, even the most die-hard hydrophobes may decide to increase their water intake!

Using wool to cover a water bottle may seem counterintuitive (you're not trying to keep the water *warm*, after all!). Wool's insulating properties help keep things warm or cool. If you don't use the suggested color yarn, however, do pick a light-colored one. Black or dark colors will reverse the effect you're going for!

FINISHED SIZE

Fits most standard water bottles

MATERIALS

1 skein of Cascade 220 from Cascade Yarns (100% wool, 220 yds) in color 7816
Set of 4 U.S. size 8 (5 mm) double-pointed needles
Tapestry needle

GAUGE

Not critical as long as fabric is firm

NOTE

This bottle cozy is a perfect canvas for customization. Knit some decorative leaves or other trim and stitch to the outside, embroider your initials with a scrap of contrasting yarn, connect two I-cords to it so you can tie it onto your backpack . . . the sky's the limit.

PATTERN

CO 45 sts. Divide sts evenly among 3 needles and join.

Knit in the rnd.

After knitting an inch (2.5 cm) or so, you may want to slip the sts to a piece of waste yarn so you can try it on your own water bottle to ensure a tight fit. Some bottles are larger than others. Knit until tube is as high as your water bottle.

Beg dec rnds:

K2tog, K3 around—36 sts.

Knit.

K2tog, K3 around—29 sts.

Knit.

K2tog, K3 around—23 sts.

Knit.

K2tog, K3 around—18 sts.

K2tog, K3, K3, then cont with *K2tog, K3* until 15 sts rem.

Cut yarn, leaving tail, and place on tapestry needle. Pull through rem sts to close opening and weave in ends.

FINISHING

Before adding any additional embellishments (see "Note" above), get cover completely wet and place on your water bottle to dry (preferably with its bottom up). Allow top edge to curl.

PICNIC PLACE MATS

BY SHANNON OKEY

These are great for keeping napkins, silverware, and other cooking utensils from rattling around your pack or picnic basket and for adding a touch of class to any picnic table. Don't forget the citronella candles for a romantic night out sans mosquitoes. (Mosquitoes really do ruin any romantic moment outdoors. Trust me on this one.)

FINISHED SIZE

17" x 12" (43 cm x 30 cm)

MATERIALS (MAKES 2 MATS; SEE "NOTE")

MC 2 balls of Blue Sky Dyed Cotton from Blue Sky Alpacas (100% organic cotton; 150 yds) in color 605 Cumin

CC 1 ball of Blue Sky Dyed Cotton from Blue Sky Alpacas in color 621 Espresso

½ yd cotton fabric per 2 mats (shown here: Amy Butler "Temple Garland" in Sky, from the Lotus collection)

Coordinating sewing thread and needle or machine

1 button

U.S. size 10 (6 mm) needles

2 U.S. size 10 (6 mm) double-pointed needles

Straight pins

Tapestry needle

GAUGE

Not critical

NOTE

One ball of CC will make several mats, but each mat will require one ball of MC. If you like, you can include stitch patterns on the knitted side (it's a great canvas for trying out new designs). Why not a seed stitch border? Knit 10 rows of seed stitch at the beginning, then continue pattern on 10 stitches at either side of the row, finishing with 10 more rows of seed stitch before binding off. Or knit a large central motif to match your chosen fabric on the reverse!

PATTERN

CO 50 sts with MC or enough to reach 12" (30 cm) with your personal gauge.

Knit until piece measures 17" (43 cm).

BO.

CO 3 sts onto a DPN and knit I-cord until it measures 6" (15 cm).

BO.

Knit second piece of I-cord long enough to stretch around entire mat.

ASSEMBLY

Lightly steam-block knitted mats, making sure edges are as flat as possible.

Cut backing fabric to dimensions of mat plus 2" (5 cm) per side.

With RS facing, pin mat to backing fabric.

Stitch all around mat by hand or machine, leaving 6" (15 cm) on short side open, and turn RS out.

Fold under and close open edge by hand.

Attach longer I-cord to outer edge of mat using sewing thread and needle, starting from center of short side.

Fasten button to center of mat's short side and attach shorter I-cord behind it.

When rolling mat up for transport, fasten closed by wrapping short I-cord around button.

RESOURCE GUIDE

YARN

Allhemp and Hempwol: Lanaknits Designs Hemp for Knitting, lanaknits.com

Blue Sky Dyed Cotton: Blue Sky Alpacas, blueskyalpacas.com

Burly Spun: Brown Sheep Yarns, brownsheep.com

Cascade 220, Cascade Eco Wool, and Cascade Indulgence: Cascade Yarns, cascadeyarns.com

Dale of Norway Hauk: Dale of Norway, dale.no

Louet Gems: Louet, louet.com

O-Wool Classic: Vermont Organic Fiber Company, vtorganicfiber.com

Socks That Rock: Blue Moon Fiber Arts, bluemoonfiberarts.com

South West Trading Company Bamboo: South West Trading Company, soysilk.com

Trekking Pro Natura: Skacel, skacelknitting.com

FAVORITE SHOPS

The following shops stock many of the yarns used in this book or can recommend suitable substitutes.

Kpixie, kpixie.com

River Color Studio, rivercolors.com, (216) 228-9276

ThreadBear Fiber Arts Studio, threadbearfiberarts.com, (866) 939-2327

WEBS, yarn.com, (800) FOR-WEBS

FABRIC

Amy Butler "Temple Garland" in Sky from the Lotus Collection: amybutler.com; also available from the author's shop, stitchcleveland.com

WATER-RESISTANT KNITTING BAGS AND ZIPPERED POUCHES

Minis (comes in a set) or pouches: Lexie Barnes, available at your local yarn store or lexie-barnes.com

LEATHER BAG HANDLES

Grayson E handles: distributed by Muench Yarns, muenchyarns.com

ALSO BY SHANNON OKEY

Knitgrrl (Watson-Guptill Publications, 2005)

Knitgrrl 2 (Watson-Guptill Publications, 2006)

Spin to Knit (Interweave Press, 2006)

Crochet Style (Creative Homeowner, 2007)

Felt Frenzy (Interweave Press, 2007), coauthored with Heather Brack

Just Socks (Potter Craft, 2007), as editor

Just Gifts (Potter Craft, 2007), as editor

AlterNation (North Light Books, 2007), coauthored with Alexandra Underhill

The Pillow Book (Chronicle Books, 2008)

If you're looking to brush up on your skills or learn more, the *Knitgrrl* books feature full how-to photo illustrations to learn how to knit and *Crochet Style* is a good resource for beginning crocheters. *Vogue Knitting* (Sixth & Spring Books) is a classic knitting instructional. *Felt Frenzy* will give you lots more information on the basics of felting, which you can put to use in several patterns here.

ACKNOWLEDGMENTS

ooks are a labor of love, requiring help from many, many people in order to come together on time and on budget. I want to thank Natalie Zee Drieu of *Craft* magazine for introducing me to my editor, Dana Youlin, and my agent, Judy Heiblum, for dotting all the i's and crossing all the t's as well as keeping me on track. Copyeditor extraordinaire Liz McGehee did a beautiful job cleaning up my sometimes tortured prose—thank you so much, Liz! *How to Knit in the Woods* was originally conceived by Kathleen Cubley, Director of Editorial and Production at The Mountaineers Books, a fellow knitter herself. I hope she enjoys the end result! (Even if I did want to call it *Does a Bear Knit in the Woods?* for a while.)

Every single day my dear boyfriend, Tamas Jakab, not only puts up with a house stuffed to the gills with yarn, projects in progress, scrawled pattern notes, and stitch markers, but he also supports me in every possible way no matter what, including transgressions such as late dinners, neglected dishes in the sink, and deadline brain. I love you, and thanks!

Extraspecial thanks are due to my talented guest designers and test knitters: Alison Taylor, Amy Gumm, Amy Polcyn, Andi Moon Smith, Annie Modesitt, Ariel Altaras, Heidi Massingill, Jillian Moreno, John Puddick, Minnie Olson, and MJ Kim, as well as to Megan Engelmann, who came through with much-needed sewing help at the last minute. Andi Moon Smith also gets singled out for her contributions above and beyond the call of duty, such as keeping me sane on deadline (a job no one would want and which she's done for me more than once). Dave Engelmann, Megan's husband, and his sons, Liam and Connor, were extremely helpful at the photo shoot and made things go much more smoothly than they otherwise could have! Thanks, guys.

Rae Nester is not only a brilliant photographer, but also a friend, and I am so pleased to have had the opportunity to work with her on this book. The models, however, added life to the clothes and objects, so thanks go to Gina de Santis, Liam and Connor Engelmann, Hallie Fagan, Ben Szporluk, Anezka (my dog), and Kevin Okey (my handsome father, who submitted to the torture of wearing a thick wool hat in 90-degree heat. (Believe me, we considered taking the ax away from him for a while.) Thanks, too, to Gina de Santis for supplying some of her beautiful pottery for photography, and to Arabella Proffer and Christine Okey for helping out at the photo shoot. No one can get Anezka's attention better for a photo than Grandma with a pocket full of treats!

Thanks to the companies who supplied their amazing yarns and to Muench Yarns for the beautiful Grayson leather handles. Extraspecial thanks to Jonelle Raffino and Katherine Cade at South West Trading Company (Kat is always on top of things for me) and to Erika Gadomski at River Colors Studio, friend and neighbor to our shop, Stitch Cleveland. Erika even volunteered her own staff to help knit some last-minute items. (Thanks, Cathy Collins!)

And finally, thanks to the Fiber League, my partners in fiber crime (ahem, *love*): Kim Werker, Amy Swenson, Amy Singer, Stefanie Japel, Amy O'Neill Houck, Jillian Moreno, Cecily Keim, and Kristi Porter. Whenever a difficult yarn dilemma calls, you're there for me!